"For the Bavarian,
life is to be
celebrated every
day anew."

Hermann Bahr (1863–1934),
Austrian author

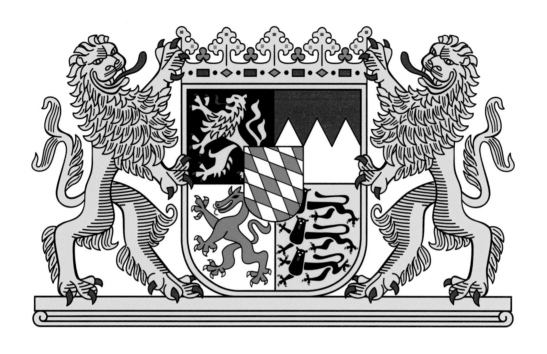

Bavaria.
Land at the heart of Europe

As if appearing out of a fairy tale, Neuschwanstein Castle rises majestically in the shadow of the Allgäu Alps. To the right, in the distance, Hohenschwangau Castle.

The good fortune to live in Bavaria

Minister President, you once said, "It is our good fortune to live in Bavaria." What, in concrete terms, constitutes that good fortune?
It's those people who make the Free State what it is – its good citizens, who every day forge Bavaria's progress with their efforts for the community and with their creativity. People like living here. Bavaria attracts them. The population of the Free State has grown in the last twenty years by more than one and a half million.

What is so special about the Bavarian mentality?
Bavarians have a mind of their own. We are fine hosts, open to variety – just look in any beer garden or wine bar. Their fundamental attitude is one of 'live and let live.' We Bavarians are full of self-confidence and get on with the job. Bavarians know what they're capable of, something which both allows us to be laid back and spurs us on to achieve more. If there's anyone who knows how to use tradition as a springboard for shaping the future, then it's the Bavarians.

So the Oktoberfest and wearing traditional costume are part of Bavaria?
Most certainly! Customs and traditions are intrinsic to our sense of where we belong – especially for the young. People beyond Bavaria's borders associate the Free State with such images, but also with innovation, successful businesses, a secure existence and a quality of life which is the envy of the world.

What is your wish for the Bavaria of 2030?
In 2030, I see a Bavaria which is free of debt, demonstrating a pioneer spirit in the digital age, a state enjoying an ultra-modern energy supply chain, at the forefront of environmental technology capable of protecting our unique landscape; a state of opportunity; a civilized state; a state open to other cultures. Understanding variety as a strength and promoting social solidarity are what Bavaria's attitude to life should continue to comprise. And if future generations say, "It is our good fortune to live in Bavaria," then we will have done many things right.

Horst Seehofer
Minister President of Bavaria

Art finds a new home.

Bavaria is a land of culture. Art and culture flourish – in Schweinfurt, for example, where the Free State financed the construction of a museum to house the art collection of industrialist Georg Schäfer (1896–1975). The most important private collection of the 19th-century art of the German-speaking lands has found a new home in an architectural jewel with, among other works, 160 paintings and 110 drawings by Carl Spitzweg to enjoy, a larger number than anywhere else in the world.

Itself an architectural work of art – the Georg Schäfer Museum in Schweinfurt.

Lower Franconia

Finding other ways.

According to legend, a bishop once refused to give the good citizens of Bamberg land on which to build a town hall, whereupon they promptly drove wooden stakes into the River Regnitz and created an artificial island on which to erect their town hall. Bamberg's Old Town was elevated by the UNESCO in 1993 to the status of World Cultural Heritage Site.

The flow of time – a kayaker on the Regnitz in Bamberg, with the Town Hall beyond.

Upper Franconia

Preserving quality.

"Malt and hop shall, by God, never stop." Beer has been brewed in Bavaria since medieval times, and always with exclusively natural ingredients. Many breweries maintain a passionate, centuries-old tradition of the brewing craft. The shiny new brewer's coops in the brew house are the centrepiece of Lothar Hufnagel's brewery.

―――――――

Bavarian beer culture – Lothar Hufnagel brews Bavarian beer in Neustadt-upon-Aisch.

Middle Franconia

Opportunities for all.

King Max II decreed, "Let the human spirit proceed unhindered," a principle which the Free State follows to this day. Bavaria offers top-quality education for every form of talent, from school education and vocational training to its thirty-two state universities. The University of Passau was opened in 1978 and now offers its facilities to 12 000 young students and researchers from more than 80 countries.

———————

Talent factory on the River Inn – the University in Passau, the City of Three Rivers.

Lower Bavaria

An eye for the essentials.

Visitors to Augsburg's Church of St. Maurice find themselves in a light-filled space. At its centre, the shining figure of Christ the risen Saviour, created by Georg Petel in 1632. London architect John Pawson drew up the daring new form of this Catholic church.

"Let there be light" – St. Maurice's Church in the heart of Augsburg's Old Town.

Swabia

A place to come together.

As everywhere in Bavaria, Regensburg can look back not only on a long Christian tradition. Against the backdrop of St. Peter's Cathedral and the Protestant New Parish Church (right), the city – which is a UNESCO World Heritage Site – has installed a ground relief, a site-specific memorial designed by Dani Karavan, in memory of the Jewish synagogue which was destroyed in 1519.

A place of living remembrance since 2005 – Dani Karavan's memorial on Neupfarrplatz in Regensburg.

Upper Palatinate

Conquering the future.

Oberpfaffenhofen is Bavaria's Houston. From here, the German Aerospace Centre directs its multi-faceted space programme. 75 scientists and engineers at the Columbus Control Centre guide activities aboard the European space laboratory, part of the ISS International Space Station.

Europe's link to the ISS – the Columbus Control Centre in Oberpfaffenhofen.

Upper Bavaria

Latitude	19.2°N
Longitude	75.8°W
Lighting	Sun
Speed	7867 m/s
Height	410 km
Perigee	407 km
Apogee	419 km
Inclination	51.6°
Epoch	2014.304.04.06
Beta Angle	-81.1°

Columbus MET
2457/17:17:30
Launch Date/Time
7-Feb-2008 19:45:30
Increment / time since increment start
#41 50/14:02:32

DLR

STRATOS

COLUMBUS
CONTROL CENTER

DLR

GMT
304/13:03:00
Date
31-Oct-2014
Munich   304/14:03:00
Houston   304/08:03:00

Band   Time to next change
S   0:31:41
Ku   0:31:41

Crew Activities
Time to next
Crew Sleep   8:26:59
Time to next
Crew Awake   16:56:59
Time to next
DPC   6:11:59

Events
Circadian Rhythms Instrumentation - Alex
Time to   4:52:34   304/17:55:35

DLR

Live and let live.

Munich – the metropolis with a heart of grass. Its 1030 acres make the English Garden bigger than New York's Central Park. People enjoy a break at the Monopteros in the heart of Munich. Added to the park in 1836, the temple-like rotunda was erected on an artificial mound.

Munich glows – View from the English Garden over the Bavarian capital.

State capital of Munich

The land

from page 24

Location

47° 16' – 50° 34'

north latitude and

8° 58' – 13° 50'

east longitude (Greenwich).

Area in square miles

70 550

the largest of Germany's
states

State capital

Munich

with

1 484 535

inhabitants
(as of 30 September 2014)

The people

from page 98

Population

12 604 244

(as of 31 December 2013/1 January 2014)
Germany: 80 767 463, Belgium: 11 203 992
Sweden: 9 644 864, Austria: 8 506 889
Switzerland: 8 139 631

Male

6 197 163

49.17 per cent

Female

6 407 081

50.83 per cent

Age profile in per cent

13.4	66.8	19.8
under 15 years	between 15–65 years	over 65 years

Unless otherwise stated, all figures refer to 2013.

The Free State

from page 158

17th session of the

Bavarian State Parliament

(2013–2018)

180 elected representatives

CSU (101), SPD (42), Freie Wähler (non-aligned party) (19),
Alliance '90/The Greens (18)

State Government

Horst Seehofer

(CSU) was elected Bavarian Minister President on
27 October 2008 and confirmed in office on 8 October 2013

Administration and structure

7
administrative regions

71
administrative districts

25
independent municipalities

2031
regional municipalities

The future

from page 186

Gross domestic product per capita in euros

38 429

(Germany: 33 355 Euro)

Economic power in euros

488 000 000 000

(equivalent to more than 1/6 of
national output)

State investment ratio in per cent

12.7

(western German state average: 9.6 per cent)

Unemployment rate in per cent

3.8

(Germany: 6.9 per cent)

"What has remained is a country that gives one space to breathe and yet still captures the gaze along not-all-too-distant borders. Add to this over a thousand years of our own history, which carries us and keeps us, gives us inner peace and a silent charge."

Professor Benno Hubensteiner (1924–1985), Bavarian historian

Schrecksee, a small lake 6000 feet up in the Allgäu Alps.

The land

Bavaria: fifteen hundred years

Bavaria: (almost) 1500 Years

c. 550
Earliest mention of a duke/
king of the Bavarians.

788
Duke Tassilo III is deposed by the
future emperor Charlemagne.

955–975
Largest expansion of the
Bavarian duchy, incorporating
Austria as far as the Adriatic
but not yet Franconia or Swabia.

1014
Imperial coronation of the
Bavarian Duke Henry II. He is later
canonized as the founder of the
Bishopric of Bamberg.

1070
Installation of the Welfs as dukes
of Bavaria. Rivalry for power
with the House of Hohenstaufen
and the House of Babenberg.

1156
Designation of the
Margraviate of Austria as a duchy
independent of Bavaria.

1180
Deposition of Henry the Lion. He
is succeeded by Otto I of the House
of Wittelsbach, which would rule
Bavaria for over 700 years.

1242
Death of the last Count of Bogen.
The House of Wittelsbach
adopts the coat of arms with its
oblique fusils.

We Bavarians emerge from the obscurity of history around 550. The poet Venantius Fortunatus reports of a pilgrimage that led him to Augsburg and from there on to the headwaters of the Inn. The traveller only made it there, however, when his route was not blocked by Bavarians. But it is not as if we know nothing about the land before the first written evidence. Eugippius, for example, wrote extensively in his vita of Saint Severinus about the end of Roman dominion on the Danube. But he did not know the Bavarians themselves. For this reason, many historians have presumed that the Bavarians immigrated around 500. Only from where? The Latin name 'Baiovarii' led them to infer that the land of origin was Baia, or Bohemia. This was immediately contradicted: how should one imagine this immigration? A column of people in traditional costumes of *lederhose* and *dirndl* marching to the rhythm of a brass band? Put more seriously, the counter-argument runs as follows: Baia derives from the Boii, or Celts, who had settled in the region along the Inn and Danube rivers before the Romans. The Bavarian tribe was formed from the remainder of these original inhabitants together with Vulgar Latin speakers and Slavs. As a Bavarian would say, *"Nix gwiß woas ma ned,"* ("Nothing is known for certain"); even today, nothing has been proven.

The outcome, in any case, is a fairly headstrong people. Around 560 we learn of a Bavarian leader, the Agilolfing Garibald I, referred to as duke by the Franks and as king by the Lombards. The differing forms of address are indicative of the defining discrepancy in Bavarian history: the Bavarians possess all the preconditions for having their own state. We still give this impression today during state visits, >

The Lindau Lion in the harbour of Lake Constance and the *Befreiungshalle* (Hall of Liberation) in Kelheim: two of the numerous historical monuments erected by the Wittelsbach kings. Tradition and history are immensely important to the people of Bavaria.

Maximilian I Joseph (1806–1825)
Bavaria becomes a kingdom. Large parts of Swabia and Franconia become Bavarian. Minister Count von Montgelas pushes through extensive administrative reforms. With a liberal constitution Bavaria is one of the first German states to become a constitutional monarchy.

Ludwig I (1825–1848)
With massive investment in the infrastructure, (Main-Danube Canal, South-North Railway), the new regions are connected to the capital. Munich becomes an art capital. Important monuments date from this period, such as the Walhalla memorial, the Befreiungshalle ('Hall of Liberation'), and the Pompejanum in Aschaffenburg. In 1848, the king abdicates not least due to an affair with Lola Montez (opposite).

Ludwig III (1912–1918)
Ludwig III accepted the title of king in 1913. In 1914, almost a million Bavarian soldiers went to war. War weariness and the catastrophic supply situation helped lead to revolution. On 7 November, Ludwig III fled Munich, ending the House of Wittelsbach's 738-year rule in Bavaria.

The Bavarian kings 1806–1918:

Ludwig II (1864–1886)
With his royal castles, the Wagner patron Ludwig II created masterpieces of Historicism, which even today continue to fascinate millions of people. His mysterious death transformed him into a myth. But under his reign, Bavaria lost its sovereignty.

Prince Regent Luitpold (1886–1912)
Prince Luitpold served as regent due to the incapacity of Ludwig II's brother, King Otto. Bavaria became an El Dorado for artists and scholars and experienced an extraordinary cultural flowering.

LUITPOLD
Prinz-Regent von Bayern.

Maximilian II (1848–1864)
The 'man of learning upon the royal throne' stood for tradition and progress. He promoted a sense of Bavarian national identity and supported the sciences as well as industrial development. He accommodated rebellious Bavarians through liberal and social reforms.

despite the fact that Bavaria is merely a state in the Federal Republic of Germany and the "Free State" is precisely not free in the sense of independent. Before the Federal Republic there was the German Empire, to which Bavaria belonged, the Holy Roman Empire and earlier still the Frankish Empire, which had more to do with France than with Franconia. Bavaria resisted the larger state entities and yet nonetheless aspired to join them. Although this sounds contradictory, it is in fact the basis for the typically German governmental form of federalism: as much unity on the federal level as necessary, and as much freedom on the state level as possible. To put it generally, politics in Germany has always run smoothly when particularism and unitarism have been held in balance.

The fact that Bavaria overwhelmingly stood for particularism is also bound up with its geography. The defining river of the land was the Danube. The oldest 'capital,' Regensburg, lay here. The names of the state's areas refer to the Danube: Upper Bavaria along the upper reaches of the river, and Lower Bavaria along the lower reaches. The settlement of the state progressed far along the Danube towards

1314
Ascent of Louis I the Bavarian to emperor. Independence from Papal recognition.

1506
End of the period of territorial partition through introduction of the law of primogeniture.

1516
Issuing of the Bavarian Reinheitsgebot (beer purity law).

1623
Bavaria becomes an electorate and a Catholic stronghold under Maximilian I.

1777
The Electorate of Bavaria is united with the Electorate of the Palatinate.

1806
Inclusion of Swabia and Franconia. Bavaria becomes a kingdom.

1818
Establishment of a constitutional state in Bavaria. The Bavarian Constitution is considered one of the most liberal in Europe.

1830
Opening of the Glyptothek, the first independent museum building in Europe. Munich becomes an art capital, an 'Athens on the Isar.'

1835
Opening of Germany's first railway line between Nuremberg and Fürth.

1866
Together with Austria, defeat in the war against Prussia.

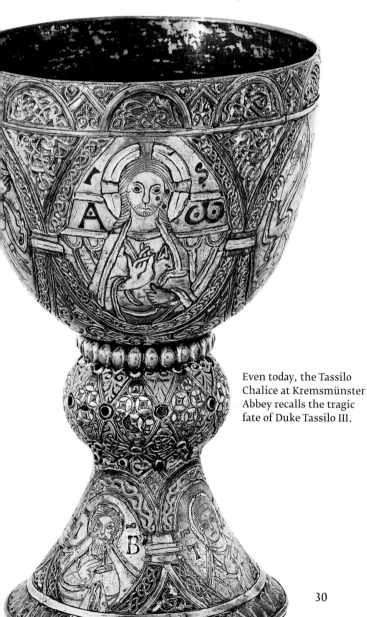

Even today, the Tassilo Chalice at Kremsmünster Abbey recalls the tragic fate of Duke Tassilo III.

The Maximilianeum (opposite page), founded by Maximilian II in 1857 for the benefit of highly-gifted scholars, is today home to Bavaria's state parliament, the *Landtag,* one of Europe's oldest parliaments.

1871
Incorporation of Bavaria
into the newly founded German
Empire.

1886
Deposition of King Ludwig II.
He loses his life in Lake Starnberg.

1918
End of the monarchy – Bavaria
becomes a 'Free State.'

1933
"Gleichschaltung" (forcible
coordination') of Bavaria by the
National Socialists.

1946
Adoption of the Bavarian
constitution in a referendum.
Bavaria subsequently fights
successfully for a federalist design
to the Basic Law.

1949
Bavaria becomes a state of
the Federal Republic of Germany.

1963
Election of Ludwig Erhard, born
in Fürth, as chancellor.

1994
Election of Roman Herzog, born
in Landshut, as seventh
president of the Federal Republic
of Germany.

2005
Election of Cardinal Joseph
Ratzinger as pope. First Bavarian
pope in over 1000 years.

2014
Opening of the representative
offices of the Free State of Bavaria
in Prague.

2018
100th anniversary of the Free
State of Bavaria.

So that which belongs together can grow together: Ludwig I banked on rural development and improved transportation routes. The Ludwig Main Danube Canal and the Ludwig South-North Railway connected the new parts of the state with the older ones.

the east to Vienna. Austria was Bavarian until 1156, which can still be heard today, for in Austria an even more passionate form of the Bavarian dialect is spoken than in Bavaria. This is no surprise, for Austria is the part of Bavaria that has managed to become and remain independent. Bavarian itself sounded in the Middle Ages a lot like Swabian. The relationships and connections with the Alemanni were close, for not only did the Danube flow towards the East, but it also came from the West. Bavaria was a southern state with close connections with Italy and France. In addition to geography, religion was also a connecting element. During the Reformation, the Wittelsbach dukes and electors made Bavaria into a stronghold of Catholicism. Even today baroque splendour and Jesuit staginess characterize our land and connect it with Austria, Italy and France.

Around 1800, the multi-ethnic state of Austria and the militaristic Prussia endangered the balance of power in the old empire. Austria made a grab for Bavaria and Bavaria stuck with France. Napoleon Bonaparte became its protector. On his initiative, not only did Bavaria become a kingdom, but it also almost doubled in size. The Swabians and the Franconians joined the Old Bavarians.

Bavaria as we know it today – with its capital of Munich and its economic centres of Augsburg and Nuremberg – came into existence in 1806: an immensely diverse land with numerous historical seats of sovereign power from Füssen to Bamberg and from Dillingen to Passau.

The new Bavarians changed the land, which now became oriented more towards the north. In 1871, when the German Empire was founded under the hegemony of Prussia, it was above all the inhabitants of Lower Bavaria and the Upper Palatinate who resisted, not wanting Austria to be excluded. Bavaria felt alienated within the militaristic empire and yet increasingly warmed towards German economic power and great-power politics. After the catastrophe of the First World War, the blame was laid on Berlin, and Bavaria first veered to the far left with Germany's only soviet republic, and then to the far right in the *'Ordnungszelle Bayern'* ('Bavaria, Cell of order'). Many sympathized with the National Socialist regime, not only in the movement's 'capital', Munich, and the city of the Nazi Party Rallies, Nuremberg. Only the rural Catholic regions proved long resistant.

Then, after the Second World War, the Bavarians accomplished what they had failed to do after the First: the constitution of the Federal Republic of Germany was prepared at the Constitutional Convention at Herrenchiemsee and given the federalist character the Bavarians had desired. This helped Bavaria even in the democratic post-war period to remain something it had always been: wonderfully different.　　*Dr. Richard Loibl*

The Museum of Bavarian History is being built in Bavaria's 'old' capital, Regensburg. The museum site is beautifully located between the Danube and the Old Town. The history of modern Bavaria will be presented in a multi-media and hands-on presentation: from kingdom to 'Free State.'

A future home for the history of the present

The Hands-On Museum

It's actually hard to believe: in the most historically-conscious state in Germany, there is no place that presents the history of the Free State of Bavaria. This gap will be filled in 2018, on the 100th anniversary of the founding of the Free State.

It will be a very special kind of museum: the Bavarian people are being recruited to help in building it – with their personal stories and memorabilia. Civic involvement is a priority in this project. Even its location was not simply stipulated; many municipalities applied and Regensburg's bid won. On the Donaumarkt, just a few hundred metres from the cathedral, the new museum's focus will be on more recent historical periods.

We will recount how the Free State of Bavaria came about, became what it is today, and what makes it so special. Legendary and unfamiliar stories will be presented on forty stages: why the Bavarian kings did not allow themselves to be crowned, how Ludwig II became a mythical figure or why resistance to the nuclear reprocessing plant in Wackersdorf (WAA) was so specifically Bavarian.

Tradition and modernity: Bavaria has long banked on this combination, and will continue to do so in the new museum. History will not only be narrated but brought to life through the most modern media technology. With their smartphones, guests can immerse themselves in a multi-media presentation of history, take a Bavarian language test and experience the origins of many traditions. In the Bavariathek, it is planned that young people in particular continue actively creating the museum and ensure that their hometowns, no matter how small, are represented. In Bavaria, it's only a stone's throw from the village to the world.   *Dr. Richard Loibl*

150 years after its eradication, the lynx today roams again through the Bavarian Forest. The Lechfall waterfall and the Lechklamm gorge near Füssen form unique natural landmarks in the Bavarian Alpine region.

The beauty of nature

At times, it's wild in Bavaria. The peregrine falcon, the white-tailed eagle and the lynx are some of the animals whose numbers had dwindled to almost nothing or were thought to have already died out, but who have become native to the Free State once again. There are over 30 000 species of animals in Bavaria; this equates to over eighty per cent of the fauna in all of Germany.

The landscape, too, is diverse. Four major natural landscape areas are united here: the Bavarian Alps, the Alpine foothills, the eastern Bavarian uplands and the Swabian-Franconian Scarplands. The impressive Alpine panorama with Germany's highest mountain, the Zugspitze, and the romantic rocky scenery of Franconian Switzerland shape the face of Bavaria just as much as the vast river landscapes of the Main and Danube and the Upper Bavarian 'Five Lakes region'.

"To them, the word fatherland is sacred, and every patch that belongs to it is important." What the Bavarian theologian Lorenz von Westenrieder (1748–1829) wrote still holds true today. Bavaria was the first region in Europe to set up a department for the environment, in 1970. Environmental protection has enjoyed a constitutional status for three decades. With two national parks, eighteen nature parks and almost 600 nature sanctuaries, over thirty per cent of the Bavaria's surface area is designated as protected. And almost a third of Bavaria is covered in forest – more than any other state in Germany.

The former Benedictine Abbey of Banz lies in the upper Main valley north of Bamberg (above). With its crystal-clear water, the Königsee snakes its way through the Berchtesgaden National Park like a fjord.

"This is truly
not a forest like
other forests.
It is a majestically
sublime forest,
which bears
no relation to our
earlier ideas of the
size of forests."

Otto Sendtner (1813–1859),
Bavarian botanist

It is one of the last ancient
woodland regions in central
Europe: the nature preserve
Höllbachgspreng in the Bavarian Forest National Park.
Here, ancient giants about
150 feet tall are still firmly
rooted in Bavarian soil, true to
the guiding idea of the national park – "Let nature be
nature" – so that these wild
forests at the heart of Europe
will still exist for our children
and our children's children.

Whoever stands on the summit of the Zugspitze enjoys a breathtaking view of the Wetterstein mountain range (top). With just under fifty breeding pairs, the golden eagle is the rarest species of eagle in Germany. The Bavarian Alps are the last remaining safe haven for this bird of prey.

"The enjoyment of the beauties of nature and recreation in natural surroundings, in particular access to forest and mountain pastures, the use of the bodies of water and the harvesting of wild forest fruits to a customary extent is permitted to all."

Article 141, paragraph 3 of the Bavarian constitution

The Caribbean in Bavaria: the Ammersee (Lake Ammer) attracts bathers with its turquoise blue water. Surrounded by bizarre stone formations and richly forested slopes, Lake Happurg is an El Dorado for water sports enthusiasts and hikers (lower right).

"We travel throughout the world and have already seen many unbelievably spectacular places. But our favourite place in Bavaria is and remains the Berchtesgadener Land district. To us, it's even the most beautiful place in the world!"

Alexander and Thomas Huber, Bavarian mountaineers

The Huber brothers, Alexander and Thomas (foreground), known as the 'Huberbuam,' or Huber lads, are among the world's best extreme and alpine climbers. In 2007, the two Upper Bavarians conquered the mightiest rock wall in the world, El Capitan in Yosemite National Park, in two hours, forty-five minutes, and forty-five seconds, at the time a speed-climbing world record (shown in the photo). The brothers continue to go to the limit today. "Our favourite Bavarian word is *'geetschoo,'*" or "I'll manage." It symbolizes in a charming way, *"A geht net, gibt's net"* – "Impossible doesn't exist."

Favourite holiday destination

A day for an excursion in Bavaria, the relatives from Canada are visiting. The Danube flows in a large bow around Weltenburg Abbey. Up on the escarpment, it flows rapidly, down here along the pebble riverbank quite calmly. A dad skips flat stones over the water with his children. Several people are relaxing on the riverbank; in the sun, there's a real holiday feeling. A long, narrow wooden boat glides through the water.

"To live where others go on holiday". From a walking tour through Würzburg's old city to the vineyards, from the Stone Bridge in Regensburg to the Bavarian Forest National Park, from the Pinakothek der Moderne in Munich to Lake Starnberg, from Augsburg with its famous historical Fugger family, into the Allgäu's Alpine regions, from Nuremberg Castle to Franconian "Switzerland" – nowhere else in the world do large cities have such storybook landscapes right at their doorsteps. Annually, over thirty million guests appreciate this Bavarian experience, among them around eight million from abroad.

Everywhere in Bavaria, one encounters people in a holiday mood – winter sports in Garmisch-Partenkirchen, hiking in the Rhön Mountains, cycling along the Altmühl River, taking cures in Bad Kissingen or in the Lower Bavarian spa triangle. Over 5000 farmers offer farm holidays in the midst of prized cultural landscapes. Anyone who comes to Bavaria enjoys their stay with all their senses: medieval castles, spectacular climbing areas, hearty meals with a fresh beer or a half pint of Franconian wine. The Free State is the favourite holiday destination of the Germans as well as of countless guests from all over the world.

Drawing strength from unspoilt nature, encountering antiquity up close or experiencing the fascination of technology and mobility – holiday destination Bavaria offers something for every taste. Anticlockwise from upper left: a view of the Bavarian landscape, Pompejanum in Aschaffenburg, Weltenburg Abbey, the Audi museum mobile in Ingolstadt.

Active holiday, sociability, cultural enjoyment and contemplation – whoever spends their holiday in Bavaria is spoilt for choice. But one thing is certain: recreational fun is guaranteed – in every season. Clockwise from left: skiers on the Nebelhorn near Oberstdorf, a romantic summer evening in Rothenburg ob der Tauber, the baroque splendour of the staircase of the Würzburg Residence, peace and quiet on the shore of Lake Chiemsee.

"Nuremberg is the most beautiful city I have ever seen; in its entirety, it is a true work of art."

Adalbert Stifter (1805–1868), Austrian author

Proud and exalted, it sits enthroned above the Franconian imperial city – since the Middle Ages, the imperial castle has been Nuremberg's landmark. The first evidence of its importance as a base of kings and emperors reaches back to the year 1050. In the late Middle Ages, Nuremberg grows to become one of the most important imperial palaces of the Holy Roman Empire. During the Second World War, the city and castle sustain severe damage. Today the structure is once more accessible for visitors in its historical form.

27 240 square miles of Bavaria

5 billion trees or

43 million cubic yards of wood annually

That's the equivalent of building a two-metre high and one-metre thick "wooden wall" each year between Munich and Melbourne: a distance of 10 250 miles.

112 000 art monuments and historical buildings

From the Middle Ages to the Post-Modern: world-class art historical structures can be found in all parts of Bavaria.

5 470 miles of cycle paths

on which recreational cyclists could pedal off at ease in 2014 along 120 different routes. With the free Bayernnetz-für-Radler-App, cyclists have the most important maps and trip planners at hand along the way.

3 915 miles of railway lines

in the Free State. This is roughly the equivalent of the distance between Munich and Boston.

More than

200 natural lakes and

1 880 standing bodies of water

with surfaces exceeding seven acres. The largest lake is Lake Chiemsee (30 square miles). The deepest lakes: Königssee and Walchensee (each 623 feet deep).

Purely mathematically, every

1.3 inhabitants of Bavaria

share the area of a football field. For Germany, the number is about two. This is a finding from the 2011 census.

1 681 miles of borders

Neighbours are the states of Baden-Württemberg and Hesse to the west and north-west, Thuringia and Saxony to the north, the Czech Republic to the east and Austria to the south and – linked by Lake Constance – Switzerland.

180 summits over 2 000 metres

At 9 718 feet, the highest summit in Germany and Bavaria is the Zugspitze, near Garmisch-Partenkirchen; the second highest summit, 9 003 feet, is the Hochwanner. Both lie in the Wetterstein massif.

49 state-subsidized plays and festivals

and four state theatres delight more than three million visitors annually.

Unless otherwise stated, all figures refer to 2013.

More than
1350

museums and collections
and, of these, 1 200 are run not
by the state but by municipalities,
churches or privately. No state in
Germany has more museums than
Bavaria.

623

breweries
There are 1 349 breweries in
Germany. Almost half of these are
based in Bavaria. Beer region
number one is Upper Franconia,
with 163 breweries. Upper
Bavaria follows in second place –
with 108 breweries.

The
252

miles
of the Main river flow through
Bavaria and through several famous
bends along its course. This
makes it the longest river in the Free
State. Its 236.59 miles puts the
beautiful blue Danube second in the
ranking of Bavaria's rivers.

45

star chefs
in Bavaria were listed in the
2014 Michelin Guide. Together,
they total 54 stars.

7

UNESCO world heritage sites
UNESCO has set itself the task of
preserving mankind's cultural
and natural assets of "extraordinary
universal value." Seven of these
lie in Bavaria:

**Würzburg Residence and
Court Gardens**

Pilgrimage Church of Wies

Bamberg Old Town

**Boundaries of the Roman Empire:
the *Limes Germanicus***

**Regensburg Old Town of with
its Stadtamhof district**

**Prehistoric pile dwellings around
the Alps**

**Margravial Opera House
in Bayreuth**

134

book publishing houses
are active in Munich alone. In the
Free State, there are 367 publishing
houses that are members of the
German Publishers and Booksellers
Association. This is the equivalent
of twenty per cent of all publisher
members in Germany. In terms
of titles, the Free State is in the lead:
13 862 titles (first editions) were
produced in Bavaria in 2013.

---

around
4.8

billion euros
is earned annually by newspapers
and magazine publishers in
Bavaria. This is equal to fourteen per
cent of the entire sales volume of
the Free State's cultural and creative
economy.

---

4 270

vintners
Franconian wine is the front-
runner: 4 211 vintners are located
in Franconia. And – 99.1 per cent
of the Bavarian wine-growing area
lies in Franconia.

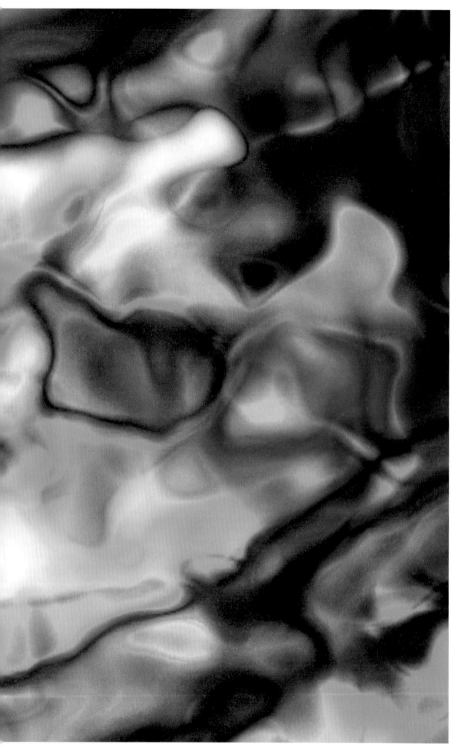

Art at every turn

6 September 2013: a lucky day for Bavaria. The well-known art collector Ingvild Goetz donates her collection together with a museum in Munich to the Free State. "It's a nice feeling to know that my collection is in good hands in Bavaria," the art lover says in explaining her multi-million-euro gift. And rightly so. In no other state are there more museums, from the Pinakothek galleries in Munich to the Schäfer Museum in Schweinfurt. The Bavarians love their art and culture.

Gothic wayside shrines, magnificent baroque churches standing solitary in the landscapes, splendid monumental buildings in the cities of the Free State – this, too, is culture in Bavaria. Not a luxury, but an elixir of life!

The Free State promotes the art scene, the independent scene, competitions and cultural activities for children and teenagers. In addition to the faculties of art, art history, musicology and cultural studies at Bavaria's universities there are also two academies of fine arts (in Nuremberg and Munich), three conservatoires (in Nuremberg, Munich and Würzburg), the Munich University for Television and Film, and two church conservatoires (in Bayreuth and Regensburg).

"Art is flourishing, art rules!" wrote Thomas Mann, who chose to live in Munich. Whoever looks around the Free State agrees. Art and culture follow the Bavarians at every turn.

Leading lights of the international art scene come to Bavaria – Thomas Ruff, the pioneer of modern German photographic art, at the Haus der Kunst in Munich in 2012 with *Substrat 21, 2002* (above). The world is turned on its head – Georg Baselitz, an influential exemplar of contemporary art with *Fingermalerei III – Adler* (right).

50

Mark Odenbach, video installation *In Still Waters Lurk Crocodiles*; the *Aschemünder* exhibition, Goetz Collection at the Haus der Kunst in Munich, 2011 (above). The only museum in the world devoted exclusively to antique sculpture – Munich's Glyptothek exhibits world-famous originals (right).

The Free State is an
El Dorado for art: Franz
Marc's *Blue Horse I* in the
Lenbachhaus municipal
gallery, Munich (left).
A Renaissance showpiece:
The Golden Hall in Augs-
burg's Town Hall (right).
Die Neue Sammlung/The
International Design
Museum Munich, in the
Pinakothek der Moderne,
the world's first design
museum (below).

No one knows exactly who the *Bamberg Horseman* in the cathedral is supposed to depict; the crown and baldachin point to the first Christian king of Hungary, Stephan I (left). Wayside crosses, or *'marterl,'* border the fourteen Stations of the Cross in many places in Bavaria. The portrait below shows Marie von Stuck, the only daughter of the Munich 'painter prince' Franz von Stuck. The hundred-yard long glass façade of the Neues Museum in Nuremberg is an eye-catcher in the middle of Nuremberg's Old Town (right).

54

NEU-SCHWANSTEIN

Ludwig II
and his castles

"The Bavarians – they're crazy. And none of them was as intensely and productively crazy as Ludwig II," according to the Bavarian journalist, Reinhard Raffalt. Neuschwanstein, Linderhof, Herrenchiemsee and the other visionary buildings of the Fairy Tale King continue to enchant us today. Visitors from every continent make the pilgrimage to Bavaria to immerse themselves with King Ludwig in his dream worlds. The flight from reality into childhood fantasies, into the grandiose pageant of art, landscape and myth – this is what people the world over long for.

In his childhood, Ludwig found space to dream at Hohenschwangau Castle against the backdrop of a stunning Alpine world. The Gothic castle full of wall paintings with motifs drawn from sagas was formative for the young Ludwig. As king, he had Neuschwanstein Castle built on the rocky hillside opposite – with his nursery in view, but even more magnificent.

The refuge and source of inspiration for the reclusive king was the King's House on the crest of Schachen in the Wetterstein massif. In the solitude of the alpine world, he lost himself in the paintings with their motifs from the Thousand and One Nights and dreamed up new projects. The castles of Linderhof and Herrenchiemsee are a declaration of love to absolutist France. The fittings included systems of electric bells and telephones as well as central heating, automatically flushing toilets and dining tables that could be lowered, like the famous fairy-tale 'wishing table.'

Ludwig II was a great patron of technological progress. He founded Munich's Technische Universität, today an international elite university and a stronghold of the research spirit and the power of innovation. In this, too, Ludwig was far ahead of his time.

Clockwise from upper left: postcard of King Ludwig II in the snow with a sleigh drawn by six horses, while Neuschwanstein Castle can be seen in the background; Ludwig at an early age (undated photo); Hohenschwangau Castle with the Lake Alpsee and Alpine backdrop; the magnificent Hall of Mirrors in Herrenchiemsee Palace; fascination with the Orient – the 'Turkish Hall' in the King's House on Schachen. The King's House on Schachen lies in the Wetterstein massif.

"It is necessary to create paradises for oneself, poetical places of refuge."

King Ludwig II
(1845–1886)

King Ludwig II had fantastic buildings constructed in unique landscapes. These backdrops were by no means only eccentric and unworldly, they were also one of the largest economic stimulus programmes of their age. Like Herrenchiemsee Castle, Linderhof Palace, near Ettal, is also an obeisance in stone to the world of absolutist France, which Ludwig II admired. Linderhof looks like a rococo-inspired, splendidly-decorated, small castle; fairy-tale attractions like the Grotto of Venus are hidden away in its gardens.

Typically Bavarian

Which symbols or objects best represent Bavaria and why? In the summer of 2014 the Bavarian state government asked over 400 000 fans of the Facebook page 'www.facebook.com/bayern.'

Wine cultivation in Franconia dates back to the 8th century. At the time, Franconia was the Holy Roman Empire's largest wine-producing area north of the Alps. The mild climate along the Main River results in wines with a very high mineral content and an aromatic bouquet. Over 14 800 acres of picturesque vineyards produce some of the very best white wines that exist, and the region's red wines are sought-after specialities. The typical vessel for high-quality Franconian wines is the *'bocksbeutel,'* a flattened, ellipsoid bottle.

> "The Franconian Rake, because in Bavaria, we will always be on top."

> "The Bavarian coat of arms: when I see it I know I'm home."

Bavaria's coat of arms is widely known and loved. It was introduced on 5 July 1950 with the 'Law concerning the coat of arms of the Free State of Bavaria.' The symbols represented on the coat of arms are deeply rooted in Bavarian history. The first quarter (field to the upper right) is divided into red and white (silver), with three white points rising upwards. This 'rake' appeared around 1350 as the coat of arms of some towns in the Bishopric of Würzburg and around 1410 also in the seals of the prince-bishops. Today, the Franconian Rake stands for the administrative regions of Upper Franconia, Middle Franconia and Lower Franconia.

> "The *bocksbeutel*, because it only exists here and is always a well-received gift."

> "Bavaria would be presented best by a proper BMW with its typical blue-and-white emblem and a whole lot of horsepower beneath the bonnet!"

Bavaria is the most important German location for the automobile industry. The two large automobile manufacturers BMW and Audi develop premium high-end cars. BMW, founded in 1916, is the abbreviation for 'Bayerische Motoren Werke AG.' In 1909, August Horch founded the make Audi – a Latin translation of his family name. The idea of using the Latin imperative form of the German word *horch* (meaning 'listen') as a brand name came from a Latin student.

> "The four rings of Audi, because they're simply great cars."

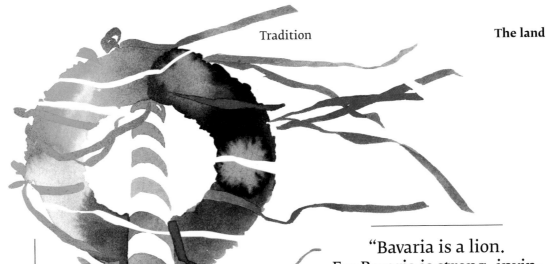

"Pretzels! The best pretzels are in Bavaria! For me, an emblem!"

Sweet pretzels are documented in Bavaria as far back as the Middle Ages. In 1318, the wealthy merchants Burkhard and Heilwig Wadler made their first donation of almost 3000 pretzels. They were distributed by a horseman. This custom persevered in Munich for almost a half millennium! In the ceiling fresco of the Heiliggeistkirche, the Asam brothers immortalized the 'pretzel horseman.' We owe the origins of the soft pretzel to an accidental mix-up. In 1839, the baker Anton Nepomuk Pfannenbrenner made a far-reaching mistake. Whereas he usually glazed the pretzels with sugar-water, on this day he accidentally reached for the lye solution, which was intended for cleaning the baking sheets. The result was so appealing that, on the very same morning, the Royal Württemberg envoy Wilhelm Eugen von Ursingen was able to savour a lye pretzel. Since then, 11 February 1839 has been considered the first day a lye pretzel was ever sold.

The first of May is a special day. On this day, in many Bavarian towns, a maypole is erected as a visible sign of springtime joy and a symbol of good luck. Plenty of strong men's hands are needed for this, since tradition forbids the use of mechanical aids in erecting the tree – which measures at least 100 feet in length – with long poles. An entirely manual operation, which frequently takes well over two hours. As soon as the maypole is standing, it's the lads' turn: they spread pitch on their feet, spit in their palms and scramble up the smooth trunk. May the fastest man win – and perhaps earn a smile from the newly-elected May Queen.

"The maypole. Anchored in native soil, openly visible, there for everyone and reaching up to the heavens. Often painted white and blue, erected by the community and inviting everyone to celebrate."

"Bavaria is a lion. For Bavaria is strong, invincible, Christian, social, and sticks together. Envied, admired, and sometimes treated with hostility. But everyone wants to come to Bavaria and secretly also be a lion."

But how did it come about that the lion of all animals became the heraldic animal of Bavaria? The great satirist, Karl Valentin (1882–1948), once expressed his puzzlement thus: "A beer horse has more strength than a lion, believe me. Try harnessing two lions to a beer wagon – do you think they could pull it up a mountain?" The golden lion in the black field of the Bavarian coat of arms was originally the symbol of the counts palatinate of the Rhine. After the enfeoffment of the Bavarian Duke Ludwig I in 1214 as count palatinate, it served as the shared symbol of the Old Bavarian and Palatinate Wittelsbachs. Today, the upright golden Palatinate lion with red crown, tongue and claws recalls the administrative region of the Upper Palatinate.

A unique backdrop for the 'Hafen-sommer' cultural festival at the old harbour in Würzburg. Even though the Eisbach in Munich is relatively small, it creates truly big waves. Surfers from all over the world come to the English Garden to ride the "standing wave in Munich." A summer evening in Munich's Gärtnerplatz (right).

"It's summer again – summer in the city."

Images of mountains, lakes, and landscapes make it easy to forget that one in three residents of Bavaria lives in a town. And many of them deliberately choose the urban life – in Munich or one of Bavaria's other urban centres in Augsburg, Ingolstadt, Regensburg, Würzburg or in the tri-city area of Nuremberg-Fürth-Erlangen. Here, they find museums, world-class theatres and orchestras, cinemas, music and arts and crafts festivals, cafés and restaurants for every taste, clubs and pubs for the night owls or simply squares and parks to sit, play music, or celebrate.

Strolling along Leopoldstraße, perhaps watching the passers-by at a Schwabing cafe and then off for a dip in the Isar river – it's hard to describe urban life in Bavaria better than the band Spider Murphy Gang from Munich. "Live and let live" – this primal Bavarian leitmotif is lived out here on a daily basis: old-established residents of Munich sit in beer gardens beside students from all over the world and chink glasses with employees of international companies. Tourists stroll along Maximilian-straße or admire the surfers on the Eisbach in the English Garden. And in the evening on Gärtnerplatz, theatregoers mingle with the young and hip from the adjacent Glockenbach quarter.

Every city has its own face, its own character, its own unmistakable attitude to life. Former seats of royal power like Neuburg on the Danube or Coburg tell of the princely glories of the past. Landshut and Straubing present old Bavarian squares full of majesty and grandeur. With their house façades and leafy colonnades, the towns along the Inn and Salzach rivers from Rosenheim to Burghausen are reminiscent of Italy. Old half-timbered buildings in Rothenburg ob der Tauber or Kronach convey a sense of romanticism and security.

"Please, no mountains, no cows. I only need the city," says Woody Allen about Munich. It's a good thing that in Bavaria, it's possible to enjoy both – city and countryside.

Enjoying life outdoors is typically Bavarian.
Everywhere in the Free State, parks and gardens
guarantee good moods (opposite). St. Emmeram
Palace in Regensburg (right) offers a grandiose
backdrop for cultural events. Young and old meet
on the urban beach in Würzburg (above left) –
just like in the countless cafés (above right, the
'Barfüßer' in Nuremberg) or at street festivals
(below, the Rakoczy Festival in Bad Kissingen).

Always brought along on the concert trips: a piece of home. More specifically, two cases of Bavarian beer. Not only the solo clarinetist Alexandra Gruber is infected by the good mood of orchestra attendants Benno (lower left) and Ivan. "You can always count on the two of them."

Benno Guggenbichler and Ivan Zelic lead a top orchestra – from behind the scenes.

"We have the best brass section in the world."

O fortunate Bavaria: with the Bamberg Symphony, the Munich Philharmonic, the Bavarian State Orchestra and the Bavarian Radio Symphony Orchestra, the Free State is home to four top orchestras. Founded in 1893, the Munich Philharmonic looks back on an impressive tradition. Gustav Mahler, Richard Strauss, Wilhelm Furtwängler, Herbert von Karajan, Sergiu Celibidache, Zubin Mehta, Lorin Maazel – great composers and conductors have stood in front of Munich's 'city orchestra' and shaped its reputation as *the* Bruckner orchestra par excellence.

Behind the scenes, two men lead the regiment; their names are not as well known, but they are no less important: "Without us," Benno Guggenbichler and Ivan Zelic know, "the orchestra could only play half as well." Or not at all – before every concert, the two orchestra attendants ensure that all the instruments are in place and that the correct sheet music is on every music stand. "It can happen that someone forgets his tailcoat," grins Benno. "And we once had to lend socks to a famous conductor. No matter what it is, we take care of it." On trips, the attendants pack and unpack up to 90 heavy instrument cases. And they always take a great deal of resourcefulness along with them when they travel. "If necessary, you also have to be able to repair a horn with a hair band," explains Ivan. The attendants are the first ones to go on stage before a concert – and the last ones to leave. They take their breaks while the musicians are playing. Then they listen and are proud of 'their' orchestra. "We have the best brass section in the world," raves Ivan. "And no one plays Bruckner like we do," adds Bruno. "At the end, when the audience applauds, a little bit of that applause is for us."

With its 2 387 seats, the Philharmonic Hall at Gasteig is Munich's largest concert hall. The city's orchestra was founded over a hundred years ago on the private initiative of Franz Kaim, the son of a piano manufacturer. The Philharmonic was the first orchestra in the world to perform Bruckner's original versions. This established its reputation as the most famous Bruckner orchestra. Ivan Zelic (left) prepares the instruments for the big performance.

Join the Ring!

Richard Wagner (1813–1883)
created the legend of Bayreuth. The Festival
Theatre was inaugurated in the summer
of 1876 and the *Ring of the Nibelung* performed
in its entirety for the first time. Still today,
Wagner's genius draws thousands of opera
fans to the 'Green Hill' each year.

Four performances, 16 hours of opera: The *Ring of the Nibelung,* Richard
Wagner's titanic vision of the ancient German saga of Siegfried and Brünn-
hilde, Hagen und Kriemhild is actually an imposition – upon the singers,
the musicians and the audience. Any yet, year after year, the *Ring Cycle*
draws thousands of Wagner fans to the 'Green Hill' in Upper Franconian
Bayreuth. The Bavarians have a love of music, theatre and festivals in
their blood. And thus it is perhaps no accident that a genius like Richard
Wagner found a sympathetic patron in King Ludwig II. Together, they
created a legendary festival theatre and a magnificent tradition. Still today,
the Bayreuth festivals electrify and polarize their audiences every year.
Booing and riotous cheers are all part of it; mediocrity and boredom never.
In addition to the Richard Wagner Festivals, many other stars also shine
in the Bavarian cultural firmament: the Ansbach Bach Week, the Kissinger Summer in Kissingen, the Würzburg Mozart Festival, the European
Festival Weeks in Passau, the Early Music Days in Regensburg, the
Munich Opera Festival, die Luisenburg open-air theatre festival in Wun-
siedel or the Richard Strauss Festival in Garmisch-Partenkirchen, to
mention only a few.

Jazz fans make the pilgrimage to the International Jazz Week in Burghausen, to the Jazz Weekend in Regensburg or to the Bluetone Festival in
Straubing. But the diversity doesn't end there: the Africa Festival in Würzburg is considered Europe's largest African music and cultural festival.
The 'Bardentreffen' open-air music festival in Nuremberg and the Samba   >

Enjoying the art of music against a grand backdrop – the productions in Bayreuth electrify the public year after year. Scenes from rehearsals for *Parsifal* from 2009 with Mihoko Fujimura as Kundry (top); impressive set design for *Siegfried* in 2013 (below); production of *Tannhäuser* during the 2014 festival (opposite page).

"Completed in Wahnfried on 21 November 1874. I will say no more. RW"

These words are written at the bottom of the final page of the score of the *Ring Cycle*. The *Ring of the Nibelung* – a 'stage festival play for three days and one ante-evening' – consists of four parts: *The Rhine Gold, The Valkyrie, Siegfried* and *Twilight of the Gods*. Today, almost 140 years after its premier, the *Ring Cycle* is still played, reinterpreted and discussed throughout the world.

The illustration shows a rehearsal of the opera *Twilight of the Gods* in July 2010 for the 99th Bayreuth Festival (director: Tankred Dorst, conductor: Christian Thielemann).

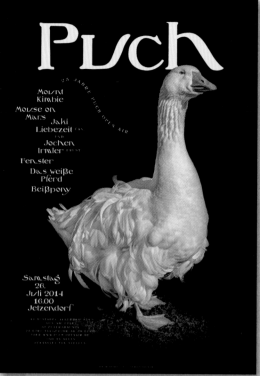

Bavaria's theatre and festival scene is colourful and lively: tradition at the Dragon's Sting in Furth im Wald (left), alternative independent sound at the Open Air Festival in Puch (poster above), top-class performance at the Munich Kammerspiele (below).

Enjoying musical highlights in the open air: this is as much a part of the Bavarian summer as the sun and the swallows. The people of Bavaria love their festivals under the white-and-blue sky. From top to bottom: *Wagner vs. Verdi* in Munich, Chiemsee Summer in Übersee, German Mozart Festival in Augsburg and Klassik Open Air in Nuremberg.

Festival in Coburg are tourist magnets of international standing. Regional events are also flourishing: soon small pop, rock or reggae festivals will be found in almost every Bavarian district.

The Bavarian devotion to theatre can be seen in the great number of historical pageants: whether the dragon is rampaging in Furth, Dinkelsbühl is saved from the Swedes, the knights are carrying the day at Kaltenberg Castle or the peasants revolting against the emperor at Kochel am See or Aidenbach – talented, dedicated amateurs make history come alive.

Around four million tickets are sold to the 14 000 theatre performances in Bavaria each year. The Bavarian theatres and opera houses enjoy top ranking internationally. The Bavarian State Opera, for example, was voted 'Opera House of the Year' in 2014 by critics in Europe and the USA. The Munich Kammerspiele has been named 'Theater of the Year' several times. Richard Wagner, for whom art was the "educator of the people," would have been pleased.

In 1903, a couple of Landshut residents had the idea of re-enacting the princely wedding of 1475. What began with 145 participants is today one of the largest historical festivals in Europe. The motto of the people of Landshut – delight the public and satisfy the experts. All the costumes and props are historical works of art. The next Landshut Wedding will take place in the summer of 2017.

The Landshut Wedding: an entire town plays at the Middle Ages.

"Admittedly just a bit of a jest!"

When the men's manes begin to grow longer in Landshut, then one of Europe's largest medieval festivals is about to begin. Every four years, the city in Lower Bavaria immerses itself for three weeks in the year 1475. That is the year in which Duke George the Rich of Bavaria married Hedwig, the daughter of the Polish king. What the chronicles recorded of this royal highlight is re-enacted in detail by more than 2 500 actors – in historical costumes and with irrepressible enthusiasm. Anything that didn't exist in the 15th century is taboo at the 'Landshut Wedding' (in German: 'Landshuter Hochzeit' or 'LaHo' for short): watches, glasses, cigarettes, short hair on men and women, potatoes or tomatoes in the kitchen. A hundred volunteer helpers are on duty to do up the city just like it was in the Middle Ages. "Even the streetlights are concealed with small sacks. Admittedly just a bit of a jest," grins Alexandra Schweiger.

For the 37-year-old journalist, the 'LaHo' is part of her family tradition. Her father before her took part in the performances and her two children have already been infected with the 'LaHo' bug. In 2005 Alexandra was seven-months pregnant with Viktoria when she slipped into the costume of a victualler. In 2009, the four-year-old was present as an enthusiastic spectator during the historical procession and the knights' tournaments. "When my eldest daughter was then able to don her own costume for the first time in 2013, she was bursting with pride." Just like her little sister, Roxane. Just one of mother Alexandra's many unforgettable memories: "The best moment is just before it starts, when this fever overcomes the whole city and everyone mucks in to make the past come to life again."

The whole family lives for and loves the 'LaHo': Alexandra Schweiger, her husband Tom and their daughters Roxane and Viktoria (to the right in the photo).

Typically Bavarian

> "Typically Bavarian is the *weißwurst* equator, because there's only one in the entire world."*

The '*weißwurst* equator' is a humorous designation for Bavaria's imaginary northern border. An equator divides an area into two parts; in this case, into a region in which *weißwurst* is eaten and another where this delicacy is not in demand. Many inhabitants of Munich consider the Bavarian equator, named after their Munich *weißwurst,* to encircle their city in a radius of around 60 miles. But this would include Innsbruck in Austria and exclude large parts of Bavaria. For similar reasons the Danube, too, fails as a *weißwurst* equator. The Main River remains – even if many Franconians would rather eat their famous bratwurst. But this, too, is typically Bavarian: just don't take everything so deadly seriously!

> "Our FC Bayern!!! Because we became world champions with the lads and they represent us throughout the whole world!!!"*

When Germany won the World Cup in Brazil in 2014, seven professional players from FC Bayern Munich were on the pitch, four of whom – Philipp Lahm, Sebastian Schweinsteiger, Thomas Müller and Mario Götze – were native Bavarians. FC Bayern is the most successful German football club and plays in the Champions League, economically as well as sportingly.
1. FC Nuremberg football club was founded on 4 May 1900. Since then, the club (known as the '*glubb*' in Franconian dialect) has played over 1 000 games in the top division. The club has won nine German championships in a club history steeped in tradition.

> "The '*glubb*' is a club with tradition."*

Bavaria has been a religiously-oriented land for centuries. Every year, thousands of Catholics set out on foot from Regensburg on the 68-mile pilgrimage to Altötting. Their destination – the Chapel of Grace of the Black Madonna, which, according to tradition, performed a miracle in 1489. Also the teachings of Martin Luther, who published his famous *Ninety-Five Theses* in 1517, have many adherents in Bavaria. With the "Peace of Augsburg" in 1555, Catholics and Lutherans promised each other mutual tolerance. The two religious denominations were given completely equal status in the Peace of Westphalia in 1648.

> "Faith. God likes it in Bavaria. So the Cross should also be a symbol."*

* Commentary on the Facebook fanpage "Unser Bayern" www.facebook.com/bayern

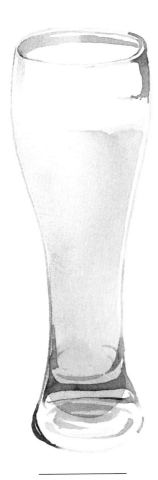

"With a wheat beer glass you can experience a nice cosy piece of Bavarian congeniality."*

"Mir kannst no a Weißbier bringa!" (You can bring me another wheat beer!) – This is the beginning of a hit song by the band Haindling. And it's no surprise, since this kind of beer – also known as *weißbier* or *(hefe-)weizen* – enjoys cult status in the Free State. Four out of every five bottles of this top-fermented yeast beer are produced in Bavaria. It consists of wheat and barley malt and is popular especially due to its aromatic, full-flavoured taste. Wheat beer is drunk out of a tall, slim glass and preferably in sociable company.

Snuff has been consumed in Bavaria for centuries, and thus part of Bavaria's cultural wealth. But, strictly speaking, one that was first made popular by a French queen, Catherine de' Medici (1519–1589). She gave her son snuff to help relieve his migraines. The royal highness herself is also said to have enthusiastically consumed it. Soon, many nobles followed her example, and *'schmai'* or *'schmaizler'* (as it's called in Bavaria) set out upon its triumphal march, first as a remedy and later as a luxury consumable. Today, the world's largest producer of snuff is headquartered in Bavaria. And the world's only museum of snuff tobacco has its home there as well, in the town of Grafenau in the Bavarian Forest. The ground tobacco is often stored in beautifully-decorated tins.

"Snuff. For snuff is one of Bavaria's cultural riches."*

"We Bavarians don't need any special symbol that represents us! What is typically Bavarian is simply the humanity and the camaraderie of the Bavarian people!"*

"The *wolpertinger*! Because it only exists here and the Prussians never find it."*

But nor are there any Bavarians who have ever set eyes on a living specimen either, of course. If at all, this shy being reveals itself only to pretty young women – if they dare to go into the forest during a full moon accompanied by a young man. This, at least, is what Bavarian lads say. Like them, the *wolpertinger* is also a sly fox, but one with the wings of a duck and the antlers of a roebuck. Or a rabbit with horns. In the 19th century, taxidermists supposedly started putting body parts of different animals together – allegedly to sell the *wolpertingers* to gullible tourists.

Produced in the Bavaria Film Studios – *Das Boot*, by director Wolfgang Petersen, has written film history. Even today the picture is still seen as not only one of the costliest German film productions, but above all a much-watched masterpiece.

And the Oscar goes to ... Bavaria!

A film school student submits his thesis and wins an Oscar. A mere fairy tale? No, it's a true story from Bavaria. Florian Gallenberger studied at the University of Television and Film (HFF) in Munich and, in 2001, his film *Quiero ser* won the Student Academy Award and the Oscar for best short film. Six years later, Florian Henckel von Donnersmarck won the Oscar for his final thesis project, the film *The Lives of Others;* he had never before made a feature-length film. Lennart Ruff studied at the HFF, filmed for three years in Munich and won the Student Academy Award in 2014 for his psychological thriller *Nocebo*. Caroline Link is also an alumna of the HFF and won an Oscar for her *Nowhere in Africa*.

But the largest number of academy awards have been won by the Munich film pioneers, August Arnold and Robert Richter. To date, their firm ARRI has won 18 scientific and engineering awards. *Harry Potter*, *The Lord of the Rings* and *Matrix* – all these films were shot with the most modern lighting and effects techniques from Munich.

The Bavarian Film Awards, the Bavarian TV Awards, the Munich Film Festival, FilmFernsehFonds Bayern for film and television funding and the stars of the modern world of cinema make Bavaria into a film Mecca. Great German films have been made in Bavaria, European film projects have been given their final touches here, brilliant filmmakers have come from Bavaria or live and work here. And the best of all: they all continue to foster their connections with Bavaria. "Filmmaking is the best job in the world!" says Oscar-winner Florian Gallenberger and, on the side, he teaches up-and-coming talent at his former university. Can you guess where? In Munich.

Oscar-winning films from Bavaria: in 2003, Caroline Link won the Oscar for best foreign film for her *Nowhere in Africa* (above); in 2007, Florian Henckel von Donnersmarck won the coveted award for his box-office success, *The Lives of Others* (left).

Meister Eder and His Pumuckl
(director: Ulrich König)
Visible only to Master Eder (played by Gustl Bayrhammer), the famous goblin makes mischief in a Munich carpenter's workshop. Unforgotten: Hans Clarin, who gave Pumuckl his unmistakeable hobgoblin voice. The first episode was aired on BR in 1982.

Kir Royal
(director: Helmut Dietl)
Being included is everything! Whoever makes it into the column of gossip reporter Baby Schimmerlos (Franz Xaver Kroetz, in the photo), has been granted admittance to the "in crowd." Glue producer Heinrich Hafferloher (Mario Adorf) tries everything, not leaving out a single faux pas in his attempts.

"There's always something to be had..."

22 September 1964: Bavarian Broadcasting (BR) is the first member of the ARD consortium of public broadcasters to open a regional television service, today's 'Bayerische Fernsehen.' From the *Münchner Geschichten* to the *Löwengrube* and *Kir Royal* – in the last five decades, some of the best television programmes in Germany have been produced by BR and ARD. Not only cult series but also cult films have been created by Bavarian directors.

Monaco Franze
(director: Helmut Dietl)
"A bisserl was geht immer!" ("There's always something to be had!") or *"Geh' Spatzl, schau, wia i schau!"* ("Oh, Spatzl, look at how I look.") Who in Bavaria does not know these famous cult adages by the eternal dandy and the series' legendary characters? In ten episodes, Helmut Dietl and Patrick Süskind depict the big-city adventures of Franz Münchinger (Helmut Fischer) and his *'spatzl,'* Annette von Soettingen (Ruth Maria Kubitschek).

Irgendwie und Sowieso
(Anyway, Somehow)
(director: Franz Xaver Bogner)
In the fictitious town of 'Zell,' anywhere in Bavaria, the hippy clique around Sir Quickly (Ottfried Fischer), the auto mechanic Sepp (Elmar Wepper) and grammar school pupil Effendi (Robert Giggenbach) experience the wild years around 1968.

Münchner Geschichten
(Munich Stories)
(director: Helmut Dietl)
Tscharlie Häusler (Günther Maria Halmer, here in the middle), charming suburban rogue with a wise grandmother (Therese Giehse), loves his city and has a head full of ideas. It's the others who manage to make money, but he's not bothered by that: *"Ois Chicago"* ("Everything's cool") – a pure, Munich attitude towards life!

Im Angesicht des Verbrechens
(In the Face of Crime)
(director: Dominik Graf)
A mafia epic in ten episodes. The Munich director Dominik Graf created a film that – according to the jury of the Grimme awards – overshadowed every previous fiction series on German television. The ARD series won the Grimme Award in 2011.

Fuck Ju Göthe
(director: Bora Dagtekin, 2013)
A gymnasium has been built on top of his buried stolen goods. Fresh out of jail, Zeki Müller (Elyas M'Barek) has no other choice but to get a job as a supposed substitute teacher at the Goethe Comprehensive School. More than seven million cinemagoers laughed through this comedy, which was filmed predominantly at the Lise Meitner grammar school in Unterhaching. The Munich companies Rat Pack Filmproduktion and Constantin Film produced the box-office hit by German-Turkish director Bora Dagtekin.

Wer früher stirbt, ist länger tot
(The Sooner You Die, the Longer You're Dead)
(director: Marcus H. Rosenmüller, 2006)
Around 1.3 million cinemagoers were delighted by this regional film that transcends all clichés – because his mother died during his birth, the 11-year-old Sebastian fears ending up in purgatory. So he does everything possible to become immortal or at least to cleanse himself of sin.

Der Schuh des Manitu **(Manitou's Shoe)**
(director: Michael 'Bully' Herbig, 2003)
Tied to the stake yet again, Ranger complains to his friend, the Indian chief, Abahachi, "I am dissatisfied with the overall situation." But the same can truly not be claimed by the Munich director 'Bully' Herbig – over eleven million cinema visitors made this Western parody into the most successful German film ever.

Who celebrates the best fair in Bavaria?

Straubing!
Because the Gäubodenfest is 'a dream of paradise.' Every August, more than 1.4 million visitors celebrate "a festival for the people, for young and old, without distinction by party or confession, for both city and countryside!" So it was decreed by the city fathers in the 19th century.

Munich!
Because the *'Wiesn'* is legendary. The Oktoberfest, which takes place primarily in warmer September, draws over six million visitors, who leave a good 1 billion euros in the city. It was first celebrated in 1810 during the wedding of Crown Prince Ludwig and Princess Therese of Saxe-Hildburghausen. The site where it takes place was named after the bride: Theresienwiese, or *'Wiesn'* ('the meadow') for short.

Erlangen!
Because the mountain summons and over a million visitors follow its call to the Erlangen Bergkirchweih. It developed in 1755 from a marksmen's festival. The *'Berch'* always begins on the Thursday before Pentecost and ends twelve days later, when the last beer keg is ceremonially buried.

Augsburg!
Because Augsburg's Plärrer takes place twice a year. Its origins can be traced back over 1000 years. The name supposedly goes back to the verb *'plärren,'* to yell or shout – or to the Middle High German word 'plarre,' the open space where the market criers loudly proffered their wares.

Abensberg!
Because the political world comes together every September at the 'Gillamoos.' On the final day of the folk festival, which is celebrated by a quarter of a million people, speakers from all political parties gather for a verbal punch-up. Even the chancellor of Germany has been present.

All of Bavaria!
Because the people between the Alps and the Main River celebrate countless festivals each year. Many are known only regionally but, for the people who live there, these are the best festivals of all!

The Kocherlball takes place every third Sunday in July. When there's dancing and clapping all around, then Katharina Mayer has achieved her goal: "Seeing the enthusiasm in the people's eyes," especially those who used to laugh at Bavarian dance. "When they ask, 'Where can I learn more?' then I go home content."

Katharina Mayer loves and lives for Bavarian dance –
to the break of day.

"Our dances are as passionate as the salsa and tango."

When several thousand people in the middle of Munich dance to first-class Bavarian folk music until daybreak, then it's the time of the Kocherlball once again. And Katharina Mayer is completely in her element. The 37-year-old is dancing mistress of this unique ball, which derives from an old Munich tradition from the 19th century. At the crack of dawn on beautiful summer Sundays, servants – referred to as 'kocherl' – used to gather to dance.

Starting at six in the morning, dancers take to the floor in the English Garden – even in 2014. Young and old, workers and students, people in traditional costumes, historical garb or torn jeans revel in round dances like the waltz and the polka, simple figure dances and *Zwiefacher*. Katharina Mayer shows them the dances, dances with them, compères and spreads good cheer. Most important to her: "Everyone can and may join in!" She was not only born into Bavarian dance. Her mother was still performing as a dance demonstrator late in her pregnancy, "I was danced into life." Later, she whirled across the parquet on the shoes that were part of the traditional Bavarian costume worn by her father, a well-known folklorist. Dancing became second nature: "Bavarian dances are simply inside me, like a gift." She was predestined to become a professional dancer. Katharina Mayer was listed in the world rankings for social dance. "I love salsa and tango. But we Bavarians also have dances that are part of us and our culture. And our dances can be just as passionate!" This was also due to the live musical accompaniment: "You can't help but dance."

Young winemaker Christine Pröstler fulfils a dream –
and founds a vineyard.

"I now make my own wine!"

The path Christine Pröstler has travelled seems a bit like
a fairy tale. At the age of 18, the young woman from Lower
Franconia was crowned wine princess in her hometown of
Retzbach. But what sounds like the end of a story marks the
beginning of a storybook career. For three years Christine
represented Franconian wine. "I was fascinated by how euphor-
ically the vintners described their wines." A passion that
turned out to be infectious. "I wanted to learn everything about
cultivating and maturing wine." No sooner said than done.
After her higher school-leaving exam an apprenticeship to a
vintner followed and then studies in viniculture. Pröstler
spent several months at vineyards in New Zealand and South
Africa and learned how wine was made there. Back home she
had a suitcase full of ideas – and a dream: "My name on the
label." But, first, she wanted to gather more practical experience. Christine Pröstler worked for four years at a large win-
ery in Rhenish Hesse before taking the next step in her career –
in 2010 she became cellarer in the Staatlicher Hofkeller in
Würzburg, one of the most renowned vineyards in Germany.
But the dream of making her own wine did not fade. Alongside her fulltime job, she began to cultivate her first vintage:
900 litres. She sold it from her garage. But, soon, this was
not enough. "I knew I had to do it fully either now or never."
The ambitious businesswoman decided to take the risk and,
in 2012, founded her own vineyard. Only a year later, she
was named the German Agricultural Society's Young Winemaker of the Year. Her next goal: to become one of the top
ten winemakers in Franconia – the next fairy tale that will
surely come true for Christine Pröstler.

Native white wines such as Silvan-
er, Riesling, Bacchus, Müller-Thur-
gau, Pinot blanc and Pinot gris
grow superbly well in the Muschel-
kalk soil of the vineyard. The young
winemaker has 135 acres at her
disposal. "I love being a winemaker.
Whether in the vineyard, in the
cellar, or during a presentation, you
always experience something new.
No day is like any other." Her wine
has been judged by the critics as
good to very good.

The carp – a Franconian national dish
Already the Romans savoured the carp as a rare delicacy – back then, it could be found predominantly in the Danube. Louis the Pious brought fish farming to Franconia in 795 and it is thanks to the medieval cloisters that the Franconian carp became a valued food during Lent and then a popular feast at the annual fair, usually "baked in the Franconian manner." Half of the table carp consumed in Germany come from Bavaria. The Franconian carp is available from September to April, in other words, in the months containing an "r." The reason for this is the lack of a cold chain in former times: when it was warm, it was not possible to transport the carp, either alive or already butchered.

Bavaria on the table: Now, that's delicious!

Münchner *weißwurst*
There's nothing trifling about this world-famous speciality; many legends and questions of faith surround the *weißwurst*. One thing is certain: it is made of veal and pork and seasoned with onions and fresh parsley.

How long has the *weißwurst* been around? The Munich city archives house an engraving from 1814 showing Munich residents enjoyably sucking a *weißwurst*. Sucking? See below.

How is a *weißwurst* eaten? Without the casing! Traditionalist 'Old Bavarians' enjoy it straight from the hand to the mouth and deftly suck (*'zuzeln'*) the sausage meat out of its casing. In a 'lengthways cut,' the eater carefully cuts the sausage deeply along its length without cutting through to the other side. The two halves are then rejoined and removed from the casing with a spirited half turn.

When is the *weißwurst* eaten? An old rule states that *weißwurst* must not be allowed to hear the church bells ringing noon. They always used to be sold raw and boiled just before being eaten, since sausage meat spoils quickly. For this reason they were always eaten before the noonday heat. In the age of refrigeration, you can eat them anytime you fancy the taste. And how good they taste, too! The singer and actor Leo Slezak (1873–1946) once raved, "I am not capable of describing a *weißwurst* because the German language is too poor to exhaustively portray this abundance of bliss."

Swabian *maultaschen*

"The best things are often found in the smallest pockets," as the Swabian saying goes. In the case of Swabian *maultaschen*, or pasta pouches, this is a stuffing of meat and/or vegetables and spinach. These 'Bavarian ravioli' are formed into squares or strudel-shapes and served boiled or fried.

How long have *maultaschen* been around? 'Stuffed pasta from Swabia' is first documented in 1831. A similar phrasing can also be found in 1885 in the Grimm brothers' German dictionary with the addendum, "usually filled with spinach."

Why are they also called *'herrgotts'bscheißerle'* ('God's little swindlers')? According to legend, it was Cistercian monks in the Abbey of Maulbronn who invented *maultaschen* during the Thirty Years War. The monks were given a large piece of meat – during Lent, of all times, when eating meat was prohibited. This is why, starved by war, they are said to have minced the meat, mixed it with herbs and spinach and hidden it in a pasta wrapping – so that God wouldn't be able to see the meat inside.

Nuremberg *rostbratwürste*

Sources first mention *'werschdla'* in 1313. They are charcoal-grilled. Johann Wolfgang von Goethe even had *werschdla* sent to him by mail in Weimar.

What's in them? Pork, typically seasoned with marjoram. Depending on the recipe, ginger and cardamom can also be added.

Where is the oldest *bratwurst* kitchen in the world? The competition is between Regensburg and Nuremberg. The Regensburg sausage kitchen was first documented as far back as 1378, when the builders of the cathedral fortified themselves here, which is why the 'Historische Wurstkuchl' ('Historic Sausage Kitchen') is considered the first fast-food restaurant in history. The first documented mention of the Nuremberg bratwurst dates back to 1419. But the 'Goldene Stern,' or 'Golden Star,' has been open uninterruptedly since 1639, which puts them one up on Regensburg. There were thus two winners in the bratwurst dispute, from which both sides profited in any case.

Obazda/Gerupfter

In Bavaria, leftover pieces of cheese are not thrown away but blended (in Bavarian dialect: 'obazd') with butter and spices into a kind of cheese spread. In Franconia obazda is called 'gerupfter' ('plucked').

How long has obazda been around? When the first beer gardens sprang up around 200 years ago, camembert and brie were just starting to be produced in Bavaria. In order for their guests to eat the cheeses even after they had matured, Bavarian caterers invented obazda.

What is in obazda? First, a large amount of camembert or brie, cream cheese, butter, ground paprika, and salt. Depending on the region, onions, caraway, and other herbs and spices or even beer are added. Cream or milk is added to reduce the fat content, making the obazda more easily digestible. The Franconian gerupfter sometimes also includes Romadur or Limburg cheese.

Pichelsteiner

This Bavarian stew must not be stirred during cooking: this is what is claimed in the Bavarian Forest. Every year, for the Kirchweih fair, the inhabitants of Regen celebrate their big pichelsteiner festival, at which around 3 000 portions are served.

Who invented it? It is said that, in 1742, a farmwoman in Regen was forced to feed the Pandur Trenck and his men. She only had cabbage, carrots and some leftover meat, which she cooked in a pot. She hung the pot on a hook (a 'pichel') over the fire. The innkeeper Augusta Winkler allegedly found the recipe around 1850 in Grattersdorf – on the 2 800-foot-high mountain Büchlstein.

Shaken, not stirred! Carrots and a lot of greens are added to a bed of potatoes. These are followed by a layer of diced pork, veal, and beef; the layering is repeated until the pot is full. When full, the pot is grasped by both handles and vigorously shaken back and forth so that it doesn't scorch.

Prinzregententorte

A chocolate lover's dream: The *prinz-regententorte* is a sponge cake with chocolate cream filling and chocolate glaze. Layers of cake and cream filling alternate, each less than a quarter of an inch thick.

How long has *prinzregententorte* been around? Depending on the source, it was invented either by the court confectioner Julius Rottenhöfer, the court baker Anton Seidl or the court confectioner Heinrich Georg Erbshäuser. One thing is certain: the cake is dedicated to Prince Regent Luitpold (1821–1912) – and the state of Bavaria. Prince Luitpold began ruling in 1886, after his nephew, King Ludwig II, was deposed. Formally, Ludwig's brother Otto was declared Bavarian king, but, since he was mentally ill and not capable of ruling, Luitpold assumed the official duties. In the more than 100 years of Bavaria's history as a kingdom, Luitpold ruled the longest, although he was the only one of the six rulers who was not a king, but a prince regent.

How many layers does a *prinzregententorte* have? Seven or eight. At the time of its creation, the eight sponge cake layers symbolized the eight administrative regions of the time: Upper Bavaria, Swabia with Neuburg, Upper Palatinate with Regensburg, Upper Franconia, Middle Franconia, Lower Franconia with Aschaffenburg and the Palatinate. Today, the *prinzregententorte* can also be baked with "only" seven layers, for, since 1946, the Palatinate no longer belongs to Bavaria.

Bavaria and Bavarian beer

"Beer is the most convincing proof that God loves us and wants us to be happy." This must have been said by a Bavarian. Far from it! It was Benjamin Franklin (1706–1790), one of the founding fathers of the USA who paid such homage to the amber nectar. We do not actually know whether the great statesman ever had the chance to enjoy Bavarian beer. But Bavaria does seem to provide evidence for Franklin's claim, for the people in the Free State – the state with the world's highest concentration of breweries – are the most contented people in Germany, as the ARD 'Happiness Atlas' showed in 2013.

Over 620 Bavarian breweries observe the Bavarian *Reinheitsgebot* or Purity Law. The oldest foodstuffs purity law still in effect was enacted on 23 April 1516 by Duke William IV: beer must be brewed only from hops, water, malt and yeast. This ensures even today that Bavarian beer is brewed without any chemical additives or low-quality malt substitutes. And that you can taste!

The Bavarians' good spirits are also surely raised by another unique tradition. In the Free State, it is a statutory right to be allowed to bring your own food to the beer garden and enjoy it there free of charge. Only drinks must be purchased from the proprietor. In 1812, King Ludwig II allowed the serving of beer in beer gardens but not the sale of food. The innkeepers had complained that they were losing their guests to the new competition. In order to sell their beer in the warmer summer months as well, namely, Munich brewers set deep cellars into the slopes of the city's riverbanks. Above them, they planted chestnut trees for shade. The perfect place to enjoy a fresh beer – and your own picnic fare – in the summer. The beer garden was and remains Bavarians' summertime living room.

"Don't drink up all your money, people: go out and buy a beer with it instead!"

Karl Valentin (1882–1948)

It is thanks to the Bavarian beer garden ordinance of 1812 (left page) that patrons are still allowed to bring and eat their own food in the beer garden today. This is a delight not only to the visitors to the beer garden at Kleinhesseloher See in Munich (above). Shady trees in the sunlight: in 1893, the Berlin artist Max Liebermann painted Beer Garden in Brannenburg (right).

Anton Schmaus is *the* rising star among
the Germany's top chefs.

"The big city is all in your head."

It took only 14 months for Anton Schmaus to acquire a Michelin star for his first restaurant. In record time, he became Bavaria's youngest star chef in 2010 at the age of 28. "At the time, a colleague called to congratulate me. I had to confirm it on the internet because I couldn't believe it." Then he celebrated – with his staff and a lot of champagne. On that day, only a trifle was offered to the guests. "We couldn't really cook anymore," grins the young chef.

After his higher school-leaving exam, the young man from Lower Bavaria studied his craft in Germany, Switzerland and New York, exclusively in starred restaurants. "Afterwards, I considered myself the greatest," Schmaus laughs. "Only then to be seriously taken down a peg or two." On holiday in Stockholm, the 24-year-old dined at the F12 – "the hottest restaurant in town." Right there and then, he marched into the kitchen to apply for work – successfully. But the beginning was hard. "I didn't know a word of Swedish. And in their kitchen, work was done very differently. I had the feeling that I couldn't do anything." The nonchalance with which the Swedes cooked influenced Schmaus. "I wanted to open a modern restaurant that could be located in any major city." But just like his first starred restaurant, 'Storstad,' he, too, located to Regensburg in 2014. "The big city happens in your head" – and on your plate. Schmaus likes to cook Bavarian cuisine, with Asian and Scandinavian elements. This delights both guests and critics. Only five months after opening, 'Storstad' received its first star. Shortly after, Gault Millau named the 33-year-old 'Rising Star of the Year,' one of the most important accolades in its restaurant guide. It looks as though Anton Schmaus is not likely to be taken down a peg or two again, but may just possibly acquire another star or two.

At the age of 28, youngest star chef in Bavaria; at 33, 'Rising Star of the Year.'" The congenially modest Schmaus speaks five languages and, despite all his nonchalance, is a perfectionist down to the smallest detail. He comes from a Viechtach family of hoteliers.

Big city flair in medieval Regensburg – not only the name – 'storstad' means 'big city' in Swedish – recalls Schmaus' time in Sweden, but also its purist design. "My restaurant is open to anyone who loves good food, whether they come in a suit or in jeans." With 'Storstad,' Schmaus has realized his vision of a perfect restaurant.

Well, look at that!

No Christmas season without **Nuremberg *lebkuchen!*** The name of the delicious gingerbread cookies comes either from the Old German word 'lebbe' (very sweet) or from the Latin 'libum' (round flat cake or bread). One important ingredient, honey, was the only sweet available in large quantities in the Middle Ages, and especially so in Nuremberg. The Nuremberg Reichswald (or Imperial Forest) with its heather – also known as the 'apiary of the Holy Roman Empire' – provided enough honey, giving rise to Nuremberg's reputation as the city of lebkuchen bakers.

The Allianz Arena on Munich's doorstep contains the **world's largest membrane shell**. 2760 lozenge-shaped panels form over 79 500 square yards of roofing and façade. The panels generate such an intense luminosity that, on clear nights, the arena is visible even from Austrian mountain peaks.

BEST PICTURE

pwc

Oscar presentation – The eyes of the world are on the golden envelopes containing the winners' names. The Oscar envelopes are made in Bavaria. The jury's reason: the paper from the laid paper factory in Gmund by Lake Tegernsee possesses "a beautifully lustrous gold, at once glamorous and highly elegant."

"Skin as white as snow, lips as red as blood, hair as black as ebony" – **Snow White**, the Grimm brothers' fairy tale figure supposedly lived in a small castle in Lower Franconia's Lohr–on-the-Main. One thing is certain – in Lohr, there was a famous mirror glassworks, but did they also offer speaking ones…?

Hell lies in the Upper Palatinate, more precisely between the municipalities of Brennberg and Rettenbach. In the nature preserve of the same name, especially at weekends, all hell breaks loose, when countless hikers enjoy strolling through the Höllbachtal, the Hell River Valley, which is as beautiful as paradise.

'Miss Mountain' contest 2014 – The almost 9 000-foot-high Watzmann in Berchtesgadener Land is the most beautiful mountain in the world. At least, according to readers of the world's oldest mountaineering magazine, it is. There were ten peaks to choose from. Heavyweights like the Himalayan peak K2 and Machhapuchchhre had no chance against the Upper Bavarian beauty.

67 houses, 142 apartments: The world's oldest public housing complex is in the Swabian city of Augsburg. The Fuggerei was donated in 1521 by Jakob Fugger (1459–1525). Just like 500 years ago, its current tenants pay only a symbolic **annual rent (without utilities) of 88 cents** (formerly one Rhenish guilder)! One of the tenants' obligations is to pray three times a day for the salvation of the donor family's souls.

Only at the Oktoberfest – as a helper in his father's electricity company, **Albert Einstein** is said to have screwed in light bulbs in the Schottenhamel tent towards the end of the nineteenth century.

The Far East in Bavaria – the world's largest collection of Himalayan plants can be found in the **Nepal Himalaya Parc** near Wiesent in the Upper Palatinate. The pavilion was hand-carved in wood by around 800 Nepalese artisan families – originally for Expo 2000 in Hannover.

The
people

"It's Bavarian to be unruffled,
to let others be what they want to be
and help them if they need it."

Stephanie Senge (b. 1972),
Bavarian consumption artist

Evening mood with
the yachts on Lake Ammer.

"Bavaria is …

...a nation of nations."

Professor Benno Hubensteiner (1924–1985), Bavarian historian

On being asked how they imagine a 'typical Bavarian' to be, an Englishman or an American might well start talking about their short leather trousers, lederhosen, or traditional dirndl dresses, or their beer and roast pork. But anyone travelling through Bavaria will soon realize that no such Bavarian exists.

The Free State of Bavaria is home to 12.6 million people, all as varied as the Bavarian landscape, be they city-dwellers in Nuremberg, Augsburg and Munich or isolated farming folk in the Bavarian Forest, the townspeople of Allgäu or villagers in the Chiemgau or Spessart countryside. Families with long traditions live side-by-side with newcomers – 'zuagroaste' – from all over Germany. The faces of Bavaria are the faces of Catholics, Protestants, Jews and Moslems, 'gebirgsschützen' ('mountain riflemen') and people wearing traditional costumes, the able-bodied and the disabled, snowboarders and skaters, craftspeople and IT engineers, indigenous families and immigrant families.

Bavaria is colourful – and has been for a long time. In the 4th and 5th centuries, Celts and Romans, Lombards and Goths encountered Franks, Alemanni and Thuringians right here between the Danube and the Alps. This mixture of peoples came to be known as Bajuwars, or Bavarians, who grew in the course of many centuries into

one people with a common language and a common corpus of Christian values and traditions.

When Napoleon and his rivals arrived at the outset of the 19th century to plough up the map of Europe, the principality of Bavaria was skillfully moulded into a kingdom by the alliance-building strategies of the ruling Wittelsbach family. Not only Bavaria was now larger but also even more multi-faceted, embracing no longer only the 'Old Bavarians' of Upper Bavaria, Lower Bavaria and the Upper Palatinate, but now also two new categories of Bavarians – the Franks and the Swabians.

The twin processes of industrialization and urbanization gradually drew all three groups closer to one another without extinguishing their pride in their respective, carefully-nurtured idiosyncrasies. 'Live and let live' became the guiding value of the Bavarians. This principle of the Liberalitas Bavariae continued to be upheld as the 20th century brought an influx of further population groups. The first – and largest – of these were the Germans who were forced to vacate their home country in the Sudetenland area of post-war Czechoslovakia by a backlash of the violence that Germans had themselves earlier unleashed. More than two million refugees and victims of this forced expatriation came to settle in Bavaria, whereupon they worked tirelessly to make a decisive contribution to Germany's economic miracle. In 1954, Bavaria's Minister President, Hans Ehard, declared the Sudetenland Germans to be Bavaria's fourth 'tribe,' thus placing them under the special protection of the Bavarian state, a status they enjoy to this day.

The late Fifties then witnessed the start of a new wave of migration by people responding to the Bavarian economy's call for anyone prepared to come and work hard. Many of those who came – be they from southern Europe or Turkey – were originally regarded merely as 'guest' workers, but ended up staying. The fall of the Iron Curtain and the eastward enlargement of the EU brought hundreds of thousands more from southern and eastern Europe. Now in the second decade of the new millennium, we continue to witness an influx of highly-motivated newcomers, both from neighbouring countries and from other federal states in Germany. All these people are welcome. Just as was the case 1 500 years ago, "Bavaria is a nation of nations."

On 22 January 1959, Martha and Friedrich Gottschalk came to Regensburg from Upper Silesia in modern-day Poland – and discovered a new home for themselves in the city on the Danube. In 2014, the couple celebrated their Diamond Wedding anniversary.

12 604 244 inhabitants

1.7

million more inhabitants
Bavaria's population has grown
by almost 16 per cent
since 1987 – from 10.9 million
to 12.6 million people.

3

billion euros a year for families
That's around 85 per cent
more in 2014 than in 2008. Bavaria
invested 954 million euros
of its own funds – almost 1 billion
euros – in childcare centre places
for the under-3s between now and
the end of 2014.

7 700

voluntary fire services
More than 320 000 voluntary firefighters based at around 7 700
voluntary fire stations are on hand to
provide protection in towns and
communities across Bavaria, whereby 25 000 of these firefighters
are women!

Over

38

**per cent of Bavarian fathers
draw parental allowance**
Nowhere in Germany do fathers take
more advantage of the parental
leave, or 'partner months,' financed
by the parental allowance scheme,
nor so much time to look after their
own children. The ratio of children
born in the fourth quarter of 2012
whose fathers were drawing parental
allowance was 38.8 per cent in
Bavaria, as against a national average
of 29.6 per cent.

More than

2

billion euros
is spent in Bavaria every year
on integration measures to enable
people with disabilities to enjoy
equal opportunities and unrestricted
participation in everyday life. To
this end, Irmgard Badura, Commis-
sioner for Disabled Persons, ad-
vises the Bavarian state government
directly. Her goal – Bavaria as an
inclusive community!

12 105

sports clubs
boast more than 4.4 million active
members of all ages around the
Free State. Now that's being active!

2.6

million immigrant family members
Bavaria is white, blue and multi-
coloured. The Free State takes in
around 15 per cent of all asylum-seek-
ers arriving in Germany. The percentage of non-Germans among Bavaria's
residents is 22.7 per cent in Munich,
17.7 per cent in Nuremberg and
17.1 per cent in Augsburg. By comparison, foreigners account for just
13.1 per cent of Berlin's population.

120 000

musicians
play in 2 500 brass music societies –
brass bands, marching bands,
ensembles and alpine horn groups.
A brass ensemble is usually made
up of a woodwind section with flutes
and clarinets and a brass section
with trombones and tubas, plus a
selection of percussion instruments
such as drums and cymbals.

Unless otherwise stated, all figures refer to 2013.

49.5

million euros
was invested by the Bavarian state government in music education and the patronage of musical culture. The figure for 1978 was the equivalent of just 7 million euros.

5

Bavarian towns
have teams in the top two echelons of Germany's football league, including FC Augsburg, Greuther Fürth, FC Ingolstadt 04, FC Bayern Munich, TSV 1860 Munich and 1st FC Nuremberg.

2075

citizens' initiatives
The 'More Democracy' society has calculated that there were 401 council initiatives and 1517 referenda in Bavaria between 1995 and the end of 2013. That means that almost 40 per cent of all such procedures registered in Germany took place in the Free State. In nineteen plebiscites, its people have demonstrated that they want – and can deal with – direct, participatory democracy.

just
50

per cent
of Bavaria's adult population are married. The highest proportion of married adults is to be found in the Upper Palatinate district of Tirschenreuth, according to the 2011 census.

19.8

per cent
of people living in the district of Erding, near Munich, are under 18. According to the 2011 census, that makes Erding Bavaria's youngest district.

3.8

million people serve in honorary capacities
About 36 per cent of people in Bavaria over fourteen serve in one honorary capacity or another. That's more than one in three. These people perform many millions of hours of unpaid work every month for the good of society.

77

per cent of Bavaria's young people
under 30 feel "totally" at home in the region where they live, while 89 per cent of them are also proud of their region. Another 72 per cent of all 14- to 29-year-olds consider it important to maintain regional customs, according to a representative study of Bavarians carried out by Bavarian Broadcasting in 2012.

Over
2000

young scientists
took part in Germany's 2014 Young Scientist of the Year competition, 'Jugend forscht,' making Bavaria's share of all competitors the largest in Germany for the fifth year in a row.

More than
5

billion euros
was disbursed in Bavaria in 2013 for child and youth welfare payments and projects.

Out and about in Bavaria

Franz Xaver Gernstl has been on the road since 1983. His film reports have achieved cult status and been awarded the Bavarian Television Prize and the Adolf Grimme Prize, one of Germany's most prestigious television awards. He has carried out over 2 000 interviews "with utterly ordinary people, with real characters, artists and change-the-worlders." So, if anybody knows what makes the Bavarians tick, it's him. "I do my best to travel around the state and avoid generalizing about what I see, just trying instead to get involved with people as individuals." But even when Gernstl does his best to encounter people in as unprejudiced a way as possible, there is nonetheless the odd cliché that really does hold up. "Swabia really did have the highest proportion of DIY enthusiasts," he said of the supposedly house-building-mad region. And "the farther south you go, the more Mediterranean the atmosphere." And how did he find the people he talked to? "My team and I usually start by going into a pub. It's easy to strike up a conversation with the Franconians. The Old Bavarians like to have their beer in peace first." The filmmaker describes residents of the Upper Palatinate region along the Czech border as particularly reticent. "You have to ask them five times before they'll reveal anything about themselves." There is one state of mind which he has encountered everywhere in Bavaria – 'Passt scho',' or "Yeah, fine," which is a kind of Bavarian version of the Buddhist proverb, 'It's the way things are.'

Jolly customs

Bavaria has the two kings, Ludwig I and Maximilian II to thank for the 19th-century revival of both traditional dress and local festivals and customs. The plan was for Bavaria to be remodelled as a state for its inhabitants to be proud of and identify with. And it worked. To this day, many, many people in the Free State love and live by their traditions.

The Red Egg Walk
Who's going to get the red egg? That's the most important question a lot of young men in Old Bavaria ask themselves on Easter Monday, as they call on the prettiest maids in the district to ask for a morsel to eat – and a red egg. A young girl hands over but one of these – to the boy she would most like to get to know better.

Leonhardi Procession
St. Leonard of Limoges is the patron saint of horses and cattle. On 6 November each year, many places in Bavaria remember the saint and pray for his blessing. Perhaps one of the best-known mounted processions takes place in the Upper Bavarian town of Bad Tölz (below left) and, of course, traditional costumes are part of it.

Whipping the Ladies
There's a lot going on in the Upper Franconian towns of Steinwiesen and Neufang on 28 December. Young men in costume go from door to door, symbolically 'whipping' the young ladies of the house with freshly-cut fir branches. This is assumed to bring health, good fortune and a bounteous harvest (below right).

Oberstdorf Dance of the Wild Men
Every five years, the Wild Men perform their dance in Eastern Allgäu. The next one is due in 2015. Originally celebrated throughout the alpine region, this custom has only survived in Oberstdorf. The characters, draped in costumes made of tree moss, leap and dance powerfully and rhythmically across the stage. Only the lichens found on tree trunks growing at an altitude of around 3000 to 5000 feet may be used for the dance (top).

Rinchnach shoos the Wolf
On the night of 11 November, hundreds of men in the Lower Bavarian town of Rinchnach hang bells weighing up to 75 pounds about their hips and move rhythmically until all the bells begin to give a deafening ring. This was at one time how livestock herders kept the wolves away as they drove their cattle from the fields to the cowsheds (above).

Whirling dirndls

A traditional flirt, whereby the *'dirndls,'* or ladies, whirl their dress-es like spinning tops, while the men slap shoes. Whirling *dirndls* is an old-established Bavarian dance not only for lovers. Many traditional costume societies keep up the cus-tom, if only for the sake of followers of costume and folk music.

Stealing the Maypole

Every year, communities want to put up a maypole for 1 May. And, every year, the young men from each village try to steal each other's may-pole. The custom is subject to a num-ber of rules, one of which requires a suitable ransom to be paid, such as food and several barrels of beer, before the stolen maypole is returned in time for 1 May.

Shoe slapping

The origins of this dance can be traced back to medieval times. A monk from Tegernsee monastery wrote in 1050 of a village dance which may point to an early form of slapping. The traditional costume societies founded towards the end of the 19th century ensured that the shoe slappers' dance survived and flourished. There are today some 150 variants of the complex dance, but all have one thing in common – the dancers all slap the soles of their shoes with their hands. Regular competitions allow shoe slappers to test their skills.

The 'Schwuplattlers' from Munich performing at the historical 'Oide Wiesn' part of the Oktoberfest.

Treasure trove of words

Servus

One of the best-loved forms of greeting in Bavaria – and one of the south German expressions also enjoying a measure of popularity in nothern Germany – is *'Servus.'* Harri Diener of Ingolstadt recalls a marvellous moment when he received a visit from an oriental sheik. "I said, *'Assalamu alaikum'* to him and the sheik said *'Servus.'"* The word *'Servus'* is of Latin origin, where it means 'slave,' later coming to mean 'most obedient servant.' The greeting evidently originated in the ceremonial language of the Viennese royal court, and spread during the First World War, when the farewell greetings, *'Adje'* and *'Ade'* were spurned for being derived from the then-unloved French *'Adieu.'*

Fei

In terms of area and population, Germany's federal capital Berlin is a good deal bigger and grander than Munich, and so it happened that a group of nothern Germans, or 'Prussians' as the Bavarians like to say, found themselves enjoying a beer or two in a Munich beer garden and unable to resist ribbing the locals at the next table by referring to Munich as a village. At which point an older member of the Munich group promptly pulled out an unbeatable trump card with the remark, "Maybe in Berlin it's busier," he said, "but in Munich it's *fei* much cosier." This little particle *fei*, which he used to lend emphasis to his statement, plays a significant role in Bavarian dialect. In the anecdote above, *fei* lends greater credence to the claim such that the listener is left in no doubt as to its accuracy. Friendly threats are frequently complemented in Bavaria by the little word *fei* – "I'm *fei* going to tell the boss about this." A survey in 2004 established *fei* as the single most popular word in Bavarian. And no wonder, considering all the ways in which it is used. "*Fei* watch out!", "Make *fei* sure you're not home too late!" or "You *fei* see that you do your homework!" are all typical warnings from parents to their children. Half a century ago, a Munich journalist managed to explain the brilliant effect created by the use of that little word *fei* by quoting the sentence, *"Des is fei nix!"*, which doesn't simply mean, "That is not so." "Adding *fei,"* his succinct formulation went, "infuses the brief statement with so much more feeling that it suddenly means, 'May I politely but firmly (i. e., condescendingly and threateningly) point out to you that what you have just said (or done) can under no circumstances be regarded as correct.'" By the way, that quotation was *fei* tough to locate!

Kren

The Italians call this plant *crenno* and the Greeks know it as *kranos*. The Bavarian variant sounds similar – *kren*. This is what northern Franconians call horseradish, used to create spicy sauces. Its ability to make its consumer sweat explains its use against fevers, colds and influenza. The word *kren* was imported into Bavaria from the Slavic area. Because of its healing powers, mothers used to hang amulets of threaded horseradish slices around their children's necks – it couldn't do any harm. The term *kren* has now come to refer to anything sour or spicy. The Bavarian expression, "Somebody's rubbed *kren* under his nose," describes a tradesman who has been reduced to tears by being cheated on a deal.

Bazi

Bazi is a term of abuse which ranks quite highly in the Bavarian popularity stakes. It is an eminently practical word which, if deployed cleverly and sensitively, can have any number of uses. It is fortunate that *bazi* sounds far less offensive than most other swearwords with their aggressive undertones. The term might occasionally pop up in an everyday chat between friends and sound almost jocular "Well, you're a *bazi*, aren't you?" The speaker is not cursing anyone here, but rather wants to express praise and admiration. The *bazi* in question has evidently done something courageous which deserves to be recognized. Maybe they are a 'clever devil' or suchlike, someone we can't be upset at. When *bazi* is intended to have more serious connotations, it is a synonym for 'scamp,' 'villain,' 'rogue,' or 'swindler.' Often, adjectives are attached, like *'gschert'* (rude) or *'ausgeschaamt'* (cheeky), to reinforce the curse. It may be that *bazi* is a contraction of *lumpazius*, a term created by students in the 16th century, who supplemented the swearword *'lump,'* meaning 'scoundrel,' with a Latin ending. On another level, the Austrians talk of a *'Weana bazi'* when referring to an arrogant individual from the capital, Vienna.

Hans Kratzer

The *Süddeutsche Zeitung* newspaper runs a weekly column written by Hans Kratzer in which the Lower Bavarian journalist lovingly, amusingly and informatively explains Bavarian terms. In the course of time, he has uncovered a veritable treasure trove of words and helped Bavarians to preserve their unmistakable dialect.

Gosche

Journalists and politicians occasionally get in each other's hair just when the cameras are running. Perhaps one of them has asked too precise a question, and the other has already had rough day; then the one lets the other have a *'goschen,'* a mouthful, a piece of their mind for continuing to grumble and trying to pick a fight. A popular expression in Bavarian Swabia describes how someone might 'get a smack in the *gosch*,' a punch in the face or on the mouth. Or if someone opens their mouth too wide and starts getting cheeky and loud, one might remark that they "have a *gosch* like a fishwife!" A woman known for her love of gossip might be called a *'Ratschkathl,'* 'Kathy the Chatterbox;' or people might remark that she has "a *gosch* like a sword" (that knows no mercy, i. e., never stops). Silence is not a prominent virtue among *Ratschkathls,* which is why it is said that when one of them dies, her *goschen* has to be killed off separately. While still alive, she might be told to "Hold your *gosch*!" In other words, "Be quiet!" The term *gosche* can also be used to pay a compliment, however. "Now, she's got a sweet *goscherl* (i. e., smile)," might be said of a pretty girl. A sour expression, on the other hand, might invite the term *'bappen'* or *'lätschen,'* describing a kind of grimace. "Shut your cheeky *bappen*!" said the celebrated Munich humorist Karl Valentin, who was himself often a sad figure who let his *'lätschen'* (i. e., jaw) hang and frequently described others as *'goschert,'* or big-mouthed and boastful.   *Hans Kratzer*

Card index boxes are piled high to the ceiling, crammed full of Anthony R. Rowley's collected notes on the treasure trove of words that is Bavarian dialect. Decades of research have contributed countless little slips of paper to the pile.

British language scholar Anthony R. Rowley explains how, despite his origins, he came to be head of the 'Bavarian Dictionary' team.

"Just as long as he's not a Prussian…"

The fact that Bavarians really do speak a dialect in their everyday lives became clear to me the moment I arrived in Regensburg and called on the janitor of the student hostel to get the key to the room I had reserved. I had managed so well up north, but down here, I didn't understand a word. The university campus was also peopled in the majority by dialect-users, but luckily, they were more willing to modify their language out of consideration for this poor foreigner and, in time, they helped me so much in my efforts to listen and learn that, in the end, I understood (almost) every word the janitor said.

My area of research at the time was ancient German linguistic enclaves in northern Italy, but I soon realized that the dialects to be found around Bavaria were just as fascinating – and still existent! According to a recent survey, around three quarters of Bavaria's population claim to use a dialect and about 40 per cent say they use no other form in their daily lives. My experience has also been that dialect is spoken by mayors, parliamentarians, journalists, doctoral students, professors and even a Minister President.

I have now spent time living in all three of Bavaria's main dialect regions – Old Bavaria, Franconia and Bavarian Swabia – and become acquainted with their prevailing dialect characteristics. These dialects are called *Bairisch* (Bavarian), *Ostfränkisch* (East Franconian) and *Schwäbisch-Alemannisch* (Swabian and Upper Rhine Alemannic). I was also fortunate in having a job which allowed me to study these dialects. Since 1988, I have headed the Bavarian Dictionary team in the Royal Bavarian Academy of Science's Dialect Research Commission. When the Academy appointed me to the position, perhaps they were mindful of the old Bavarian saying, "Just as long as he's not a *Preiss*, a Prussian." I should perhaps add that I also have the support of three real Bavarians on my editorial team. Dialects are an incredibly fascinating phenomenon for language scholars when one begins to see how they reflect the entire history of a community. Gothic, Latin, Czech, Italian and French loan-words bear living testimony to the real-life encounters of Bavarians with Gothic, Roman, Czech, Italian and French (and other, more minor) language groups. The term *'maut,'* for 'toll,' originally used as a dialect word in Bavaria and Austria before gaining its current nationwide recognition as part of a political agenda, actually developed from a term used by the old Goths on the Black Sea, while a *'potschamperl,'* or chamber pot, mutated in common parlance from the French *'pot de chambre.'*

A dialect can be defined in terms of its accent, intonation, grammar and vocabulary. Essentially, every single village has its own idiolect, while larger dialect areas can be distinguished along isoglosses according to phonetic rules. As my principle occupation is to create a dialect dictionary, it is the vocabulary which attracts my attention most. I am often asked if I have a favourite item of vocabulary, but the simple fact is that I like them all – in particular, of course, the ones I myself am working on at any given time for our Bavarian Dictionary. Currently, that word is *'bub,'* cognate with 'boy.' Just as important, naturally, is the word *'mädchen,'* for maiden, or girl. The Bavarian dialect terms used for this immediately betray the origins of the speaker. Someone talking of a young female using the term *'a diandl'* or *'a deandl'* is recognizably from Upper or Lower Bavaria. In Munich or Franconia, you are more likely to hear *'a madl'* – not to be confused with the Lower Franconian variation, *'määdle.'* Someone from Old Bavaria living north of the Danube, perhaps from the Upper Palatinate, can be heard to say *'a moidl,'* while the people in the southern Bavarian Forest will talk of *'a mesch,'* which derives from *'mensch,'* the word for 'person.' And then there are those in Allgäu who say *'a fehl,'* the term deriving from the Latin *'filia.'* All of which are fortunately only examples of linguistic and not anatomical distinctions. The various isoglosses have emerged by virtue of contact between two areas having been suspended and thus reflect, even to this day, medieval territorial and parish boundaries.

Professor Anthony R. Rowley
is British and has dedicated himself to research into the Bavarian language. He works with a large team of helpers on a Bavarian Dictionary for the Royal Bavarian Academy of Sciences. A job for life, as Professor Rowley has now been working on the project for a quarter of a century, and there's still around fifty years of research to be done before the volume is complete.

Land submerged: The flood of 2013 caused 1.3 billion euros worth of damage. The water level in Passau stood at 39 feet above normal, the highest since medieval times.

'Passau Clears Up' – Flood relief 2.0

"Helping was the most natural thing in the world for us."

For days and days in June 2013, the heavens opened over every corner of Bavaria. Whole towns and villages were submerged. One town particularly badly hit was Passau, which lies at the confluence of the Danube, Inn and Ilz rivers. When the millennial floods subsided, the city lay buried under a sea of mud and debris. Then, just barely a week later, the most pressing clearing-up tasks had already been concluded, all thanks to four young people – Karoline Oberländer, Lisa Wagner, Dorothea Will and Manuel Grabowski – who now recall that they "wanted to help like a lot of people did, and the challenge was how to get relief workers to where they were most needed."

The four students and employees at Passau University spontaneously set up a Facebook page called *'Passau räumt auf,'* or 'Passau Clears Up.' In a matter of hours, thousands of people had registered to offer help and, overnight, the department office of the Philosophy Faculty was transformed into the co-ordination centre for these civilian helpers. "We arranged with the official emergency relief services how to coordinate our 5000 volunteers." The moment an area was declared safe, the helpers got down to work, shovelling mud, emptying cellars and digging the city out from under the debris; the 'Passau Clears Up' team also organized any heavy-duty equipment needed and all the catering. And they were successful. "The chief fire officer in charge confirmed that our volunteers managed more on the first day alone than was done in the whole of the first fortnight after the floods of 2002." A little idea that had huge consequences, being emulated all over Europe. "We are still being regularly invited to give talks on what we learned."

Lisa Wagner, Dorothea Will, Karoline Oberländer and Manuel Grabowski received the German *Bürgerpreis* citizens' award in 2013 for what their 'Passau Clears Up' campaign achieved. The warmest praise came from those directly affected. "These students are what make Passau rich." Not forgetting the countless members of voluntary fire brigades and other relief organizations who worked night and day to help.

"People with disabilities must be in a position to participate in society. They should enjoy the same rights and opportunities as people without disabilities. They must be able to go anywhere and join in with anything."

Excerpt from the Bavarian Plan of Action for the Implementation of the UN Convention on the Rights of Persons with Disabilities

Swinging on high between the treetops – wheelchair users can try it, too! The Rummelsberg forest rope park in Schwarzenbruck near Nuremberg provides treetop double-rope courses under the supervision of specially-trained coaches. Inclusion is also writ large elsewhere – the neighbouring hotel and restaurant employ people with disabilities in all departments. Which is why the Forest Rope Park was awarded the 2014 Bavarian *Miteinander* (*'Together'*) Prize for its efforts to promote inclusion.

Three women, three violins and one man on the double bass – 'Zwirbeldirn' are a hit not only at the 'Oide Wiesn' (Old Meadow) historical corner of the Munich *Oktoberfest* (top). A flugelhorn as played by the 'Kofelgeschroa' quartet (left). The 'Josef Menzl Kapelle' band has been playing wind instrumental music successfully since 1995 (bottom).

Folk music bridging tradition und global entertainment

The sound of home

They call themselves 'Zwirbeldirn,' 'Kofelgeschroa,' 'BoXgalopp' or 'Luderleabe' and come from every corner of Bavaria. And they are all great musicians! They know what power and energy lies in the music of their home country and have long since discovered how trendy and rousing such music can be! Since the 1980s, talented musicians have been integrating their local musical traditions into current developments in the international youth music scene. In the early days, there were just the 'Biermosl Blosn,' the 'Mehlprimeln,' 'Bavario' or the 'Fraunhofer Saitenmusik,' but from the 1990s onwards, the movement gathered steam. Soon, a wider public began to listen to this mix of regional and international music. It is not at all easy to put a label on the genre, which is variously referred to as 'TradiMix,' 'VolXmusik,' (whereby the X symbolizes the crossover) or 'Neue Volksmusik.'

The early years witnessed the establishment of the folk music of the alpine region as the basis for the musical embrace of jazz, folk, punk, hip hop, disco or just music from other cultural circles. The trend has in the meantime developed into a style of its own. Ensembles such as 'Haindling,' 'Django 3000,' the 'CubaBoarischen' and, of course, 'LaBrassBanda' make successful appearances at major venues within and beyond the boarders of Bavaria. Dressed in *lederhose* and T-shirts, playing dulcimer and saxophone, rapping and yodelling in coarse Bavarian dialect, these groups present the music of their home regions 'in modern dress' to a young urban audience. Melodies and lyrics handed down through generations are skillfully dissected and reassembled within a framework of new rhythms and chord patterns, allowing these performers to distinguish themselves from the middle-of-the-road German-language folk hits.

The music seems to appeal to everybody – well, nearly everybody – from typical true-blooded Bavarians to clubbing youths, bridging the generations and far removed from worn-out stereotypes and seeming, well, just somehow authentic. In addition to dedicated radio and television platform formats, the genre has its own live festivals like the 'Fraunhofer Volksmusiktage' in Munich, 'drumherum – das Volksmusikspektakel' in the Lower Bavarian town of Regen, 'Antistadl' in Bamberg, the 'Heimatsound Festival' at Oberammergau's Passion Play theatre or the 'Mundart Festival' of dialect music in the Upper Palatinate. All of them have already earned enthusiastic comments on Facebook and YouTube like *"Voixmusi is cool!"*   *Roland Pongratz*

'LaBrassBanda' from Übersee on Lake Chiemsee perform bare-footed rock with Bavarian lyrics at Europe's biggest music festivals (top). The Franconian band 'Kellerkommando' combine the traditional and the modern with electro-beats, wind instruments and traditional dialect (bottom).

19-year-old Leon Weber is one of the world's most
successful remix producers

"I had an enquiry recently from Lenny Kravitz."

To get out of learning, you can always tidy up your room. Or maybe write a worldwide hit. It was April 2013, and instead of cramming for his *Abitur* school-leaving exams, 18-year-old Leon Weber took his mind off his schoolwork by trying out some music software friends had recently given him which allows existing songs to be reworked. He set about remixing a number by the British indie folk group, 'Daughter.' "I just sat down and tried a few things out." Four days later, he put his first composition on-line. It took less than twenty-four hours for an influential French blogger to pick up on the piece and put it on his website. In no time at all, the song had received millions of clicks – and a certain Munich schoolboy was now a world-famous remix producer.

What may have seemed like a lucky shot was actually the product of a great deal of ability. Leon Weber grew up in a musical family. "My mother sat me at the piano before I could really talk." In younger years, he played the cello in Germany's national youth orchestra, winning second prize in this category at the *Jugend musiziert* national youth music festival in 2010. "As you would expect, a classical background definitely helps when you're remixing. I find it very easy to hear what chords will fit and how you can create an attractive timbre."

Leon Christoph Alexander Weber has moved on from his first hit and now goes by the name of DJ LCAW, his initials. He has made successful appearances as a DJ in Paris, Brussels and Berlin. And he has upcoming dates in Shanghai, New York and Los Angeles. His new tracks have also attracted millions of clicks, with established musicians now directly asking him to remix their songs. The last enquiry was from Lenny Kravitz. Despite the success, Leon didn't forget to finish his schooling. "But the final grade is my secret!"

"At a classical concert, the audience listen in silence, but when I start DJ-ing, they all begin to erupt and get caught up in my rhythm – what a cool feeling!" Not that Leon Weber has any plans to forget his classical music; he wants to combine it with his electro sounds.

"Within me
beats the heart of
a Bavarian."

Former
Pope Benedict XVI.

On 19 April 2005, Cardinal
Joseph Ratzinger became the
first Bavarian pope in over
1 000 years. Before he became
Benedict XVI and succes-
sor to John Paul II, Ratzinger,
born in Marktl on the Inn,
was a professor of theology
in Regensburg and Arch-
bishop of Munich. On 28 February 2013, Pope Bene-
dict XVI relinquished the
Papacy and has since lived
as emeritus pope.

From top to bottom: Destination for pilgrims from all over the world – the Black Madonna in the Chapel of Mercy in Altötting; a Catholic Corpus Christi procession in Fischbachau; Munich's new main synagogue, Ohel Jakob; the prayer hall in the Hijra mosque in Lauingen on the Danube.

Bavaria sancta – where the church is the heart of the village

How to begin? Perhaps with the *Patrona Bavariae,* the mother of God, to whom Elector Maximilian I dedicated the land in a document written in his own blood? Or with the countless wayside crosses and chapels, shrines and pilgrim paths that criss-cross mountain and valley like the sinews in a juicy steak? Or how about a simple *"Grüß Gott,"* the standard greeting in Bavaria?

The idea of *Bavaria sancta,* the spiritual place that is Bavaria, is more than just a phrase, especially when we look at the baroque and rococo buildings that are everywhere in evidence, from the royal court buildings in the capital to the little chapel in the farthest corner of the state. Nowhere in Germany has Christianity made a clearer imprint on the lives of ordinary people than in Bavaria. On its culture, its traditions, its language and even in the appearance of its landscape – and not least in the dialectic realm of thought, where Bavarians, to the astonishment of others, effortlessly assimilate the physical and the metaphysical as if divinely inspired.

Perhaps the most lasting development aid of all time was provided by Irish and Scottish monks who came to re-focus the Christian church in Bavaria in the 8th century. *Terra benedicta:* what had hitherto been wasteland was now cleared, cultivated and blessed with Benedictine schools, hospitals and rudimentary medical care. 739 AD saw the drafting of Bavaria's ecclesiastical order and thus the first regional church on German soil, this effectively being Bavaria's entry into the Europe of the Church of Rome. The natural affinity felt to those in

the Roman south made the step an easier one to take, while the Bavarians' unbridled temperament was amenable to the gaily sensual focus of the Catholic faith. It made little difference that bishops pleaded with their flocks to sing the litany with a greater degree of awe and respect, and less 'rustically.' Oscar Maria Graf praised the "artful, even waggish humorousness " in the "irrepressibly juicy lust for life" evident in Bavaria's churches. Popular religion was expressed "crudely, directly and devoid of any respect." And yet, simultaneously, perfectly seriously, sincerely, faithful to the Word received. A bit sloppily, too, of course, and we all know God occasionally turns a blind eye anyway. "Had it been any different," Graf summed up, "we could never have ended up as Catholics."

The liturgical calendar, with Easter and the harvest festival, sets the rhythm, while the church bell sets the time. When the midday Angelus bells ring out, it is time to down the scythe; Sunday is not to be a day of sweat and grind. The village church is open to abuse, but if it were not there, the village would have no spiritual middle and thus no true heart. Here is something which makes you stop and think, and meditate on what is right and what is wrong, and tells you not to interfere. Live and let live. It's known as the *Liberalitas Bavariae,* Bavaria's heartfelt broad-mindedness.

The variety that is Bavaria also encompasses the Protestant contribution. There are some 2.6 million Lutherans living in the Free State. The Reformation drove relentlessly south from the Spessart uplands to the Karwendel Alps, seizing on the rotting remains of monastic secularization, sales of indulgences and a clergy in decay. In the *Confessio Augustana* of 1530, towns like Nuremberg swore their allegiance to Lutheranism. The Protestant faith now began to contribute to the regeneration of the region's foundations and became – just like Jewish culture – an important component in Bavaria's development, both in Franconia and beyond.

Much has changed. The Free State has, as elsewhere, not remained unaffected by the loss of faith and religious solidarity since. The blood flowing through the state's veins, Bavaria's identity and the credo underlying the way of life that makes it so admired the world over, still continue to draw on ancient religious sources. The state even managed to produce a pope at the outset of the new millennium. Benedict XIV, a self-declared Bavarian patriot and lover of all things genuinely Bavarian, lost no time in adding the anthem of his home country to the Roman Catholic book of prayer. "God be with you, Bavarian state" may now, on the highest authority, be belted out at every service on the planet and has thus, in a way, become a worldwide hit. *Peter Seewald*

From top to bottom: So many forms of piety: the pilgrimage Basilica of the Fourteen Holy Helpers near Bad Staffelstein in Upper Franconia; a farmhouse family altar; the Protestant Gethsemane Church in Würzburg.

Franz Stangassinger makes *lederhosen* –
to measure and with passion

Christine, a Stangassinger apprentice,
painting a *lederhose* using a blue dye made
from logwood bark. The *lederhose* is then
embroidered by hand with mulberry silk.
The colour scheme used for the embroidery
reveals the wearer's origins – pale green
is for Berchtesgaden, moss green for Reit
im Winkl and yellow for Munich.

"Just hold out your hand and feel the difference."

Any self-respecting man in Bavaria simply must have a *'hirschlederne,'* a pair of deerskin short trousers. And even outside Bavaria, more and more men are having a pair made to measure, recounts master currier Franz Stangassinger. "My customers arrive from Singapore and New York on their private jets." Which makes it hard to believe that the craft would have all but died out in the 1960s, had it not been for Stangassinger's father, who fought to be allowed to learn the craft of making leather trousers. There are currently five such coarse-leather curriers in Bavaria, and they were all apprenticed to Franz Stangassinger or his father.

A lot of work goes into a good pair of *lederhosen.* The 44-year-old needs 30 hours for each pair, and turns out 300 a year, each pair a one-off. Anyone wanting a handmade pair of deerskin trousers has to wait at least eighteen months, regardless of name or purse. "Some offer me more money to deliver sooner, but I treat all my customers the same, otherwise I couldn't look them in the eye." Since his Berchtesgaden atelier opened in 1888, the Good and the Great have been regular customers. Empress Elisabeth, known as 'Sissi,' came here to buy her leather riding breeches, and the Bavarian Royals came for their *'krachledernen,'* or leather shorts. And they're the ones who really made the *lederhose* popular." And just why are they so in vogue again today? "When you wear a *lederhose,* you always look smart," Stangassinger explains. He himself never wears anything else, whether he's working, hiking or going to church. "People want healthy, natural textiles, none of that poisonous junk. Just hold out your hand and feel the difference right away." Demand is on the rise, and the Berchtesgaden craftsman could doubtless expand his business. "Expand? What for? I live perfectly well from my work and am quite content with what I already have."

Christina Kronawitter (bottom right) puts her whole heart into her creations. Her line also includes classical *dirndl* dresses (top). If the wearer ties the bow around the front of her waist knotting it to the left, she reveals that she is still 'available,' while a bow knotted to the right says she is already taken.

Christina Kronawitter combines traditional dress with streetwear style.

"Retro, romantic or a bit o' rock."

As early as the Nineties, Christina Kronawitter would go to school in a typically Bavarian *lederhose* or a traditional *dirndl* dress. "Everybody used to say, 'Well, look at you!'" Nowadays, it's perfectly normal for the Free State's young people to don the traditional clothing of their home country. This trend is supported by a whole host of young fashion designers who mix traditional dress with modern elements, in some cases completely reinterpreting conventional styles. The 37-year-old Kronawitter is one of them, and runs a boutique in the Lower Bavarian town of Straubing. "I would describe my style as retro-Bavarian streetwear. I use tried and tested fabrics and combine modern and classical lines." In this respect, she is following in a Bavarian tradition – long ago, a *dirndl* dress would be handed down from generation to generation, always being done up again a little bit. The busy Lower Bavarian searches through flea markets or wherever she travels, and asks around among her friends for old bedding, tablecloths or curtains to be used in the making of her unique dirndls, skirts, dresses and tops.

But is it really permissible to do that, effectively changing the whole purpose of a *dirndl*? "Originally, a *dirndl* was the working attire of maids and farmers' wives. It was only in the early 19th century that it began to be noticed by the womenfolk in the towns. Strict rules on how to wear one do not exist," the fashion designer explains. The Lower Bavarian is pleased to see that "when I go into town wearing a traditional *dirndl* or one of my dresses, I often hear people remarking on how smart I look and that they'd like one just the same!" Whether the style is retro, romantic or a bit rock'n'roll, "there's a new free spirit prevailing with regard to traditional costume. The idea behind my designs is to express a positive feeling – be cool, be Bavarian!"

A matter of opinion!

What characterizes Bavaria and the Bavarians? Bavaria's state government wanted to know and people in the Free State and from around the world were asked. Their opinions were added to historically-recorded opinions and the result is, well, a matter of opinion!

"They are vainglorious, hot-tempered and intemperate, yet they are neither unreliable nor dishonest."

Michel de Montaigne (1533–1592),
French philosopher

"The human warmth that Bavarians radiate!!! And me, an immigrant, I feel welcome!!! Thank you, Bavaria. Like!!!"*

"The Bavaria I know is broad-minded, liberal, a tad crazy and, all in all, the best mix there is!"*

"Of course, I'm not a human. I'm Bavarian."

Karl Valentin (1882–1948),
Munich comedian,
writer and actor

"Live and let live – that's the Bavarian way. Bavarians are traditionally-minded and rooted in the soil. They love their home country, the countryside, the culture, and they show it, too."

Franz Beckenbauer (b. 1945),
Bavarian footballing legend and honorary president of FC Bayern Munich; winner of many awards, including the Bavarian Sports Prize

"Bavaria is where I became what I am, starting at Munich's intimate theatre, the Kammerspiele, before doing a lot for Bavarian Television and everything was lovely. Whenever I finish a theatre engagement in Hamburg and travel down past Würzburg, I feel I can almost taste the sausages and sauerkraut. If there's any nation or group of people I feel I belong to, then it's the Bavarians."

Ruth Maria Kubitschek (b. 1931),
German actress and writer, known for her role as *Spatzl* in the 1980s cult series Monaco Franze; winner of many awards, including the Bavarian Television Prize

"Bavaria's a wonderful place you can always go and visit, and it's the only place where my status is Prussian. Prussia disappeared in 1947 and so did the Prussians, but any non-Bavarian venturing into Bavaria undergoes this transformation into a Prussian."*

The people of Bavaria drink a great deal, they have lots of children, and are maybe a bit less friendly and a bit more headstrong than other people who just stay at home and grow old."

John Turmair of Abensberg, known as Aventinus, (1477–1534),
humanist father of Bavarian history-writing

"Heads are bigger in Bavaria than elsewhere."

Robert Nuslan,
Chairman of Hutkönig hatmakers in Regensburg; Hutkönig produce hand-made hats for clients including Pope Benedict XIV and Hollywood

---

"Pride in your home country, your undying loyalty to it and a high degree of identification with Bavarian tradition. I write this as the happily-married Prussian husband of an Allgäu girl!"*

*Commentary on the Facebook fanpage "Unser Bayern" www.facebook.com/bayern

"Bavaria has many friends and admirers in Québec. We actually share a remarkably similar fate – a profoundly Catholic social history, developing from an agricultural economy into a brilliant, technological society. And not forgetting that even if Bavaria produced a pope, well, Québec nearly did, too!"

Bernard Landry (b. 1937),
Canadian politician
and former Prime Minister
of Québec

"I grew up in Würzburg and will always sense my Bavarian roots. Every summer, I come home for a few weeks, and the moment I enter the door, I'm that little boy Dirk again, my parents' son. Even today, my mother gives me pocket money when I'm in Würzburg. I like spending my time with my family and friends."

Dirk Nowitzki (b. 1978),
NBA basketball player and "one of the greatest players of all time," according to Earvin "Magic" Johnson; winner of many awards, including the Bavarian Sports Prize

"I am a Prussian living in Bavaria. And because I am a bridge-builder by nature, I am also a Prussian Bavarian. When I travel through the Alpine foreland region and see the mountains rising like bluish-dark clouds on the horizon, then I can think of nothing more beautiful. Then I am in a land that really was created by God on a Sunday, and I am moved."

Armin Mueller-Stahl (b. 1930),
German actor, musician, painter and writer, awarded the Bavarian Film Prize for his life's work

"Bavaria may well be the only state in Germany which, by virtue of its material importance, unmistakable tribal idiosyncrasy and the skilled leaders to have blessed it, has succeeded in forming a true and self-satisfying sense of nationhood."

**Otto von Bismarck
(1815–1898),**
Germany's first Imperial
Chancellor

"For me, Bavaria is one of the economic capitals of the world – it amazes me how many world leaders can be found in an area of this size!"

Morgana von Niekerk,
born on the Rhine,
she has been living in South
Africa for the last 23 years

"When the time comes to rest, the Bavarian hates to rest; when his work is done, the Bavarian enjoys nothing more than doing more work."

Lorenz von Westenrieder (1748–1829),
Bavarian writer and historian

"The Bavarian you see is the Bavarian you get. Never anything else." *

"To me, Bavaria means home, where I feel alive and inspired."

Magdalena Neuner (b. 1987),
world-beating Bavarian biathlon star and double Olympic champion; winner of many awards, including the Bavarian Sports Prize

"A happy, optimistic race of people, probably the most artistically gifted of all Germans."

Hans Thoma (1839–1924), German painter

Bavaria, the land of artists. As it has always been. The Humanist and Renaissance periods saw the emergence of immortal geniuses – Hans Holbein the Elder in Augsburg, Albrecht Dürer in Nuremberg. Dürer's paintings and engravings were sought after by the richest merchants and most powerful rulers of his day.

And then there were the Asam brothers, Cosmas Damian and Egid Quirin, who created masterpieces. Their work as sculptors, plasterers and painters lent a breathtaking beauty to Bavaria's churches. Churchgoers would be met by a rococo splendour otherwise known only to princes in the most magnificent of castles and palaces. Freising Cathedral, St. Emmeram's Abbey in Regensburg or Weltenburg Abbey – all decorated with a monumental pictorial language of faith.

Another language universally understood is the language of music. Folk music, for example, is usually regarded as the national language of Bavaria. It is no surprise that Bavaria has produced such great composers and standard-bearers of modern music as Munich's Carl Orff and Richard Strauss. The 'Sunrise' introduction to Strauss' symphonic poem, 'Thus spoke Zarathustra' is without doubt one of the world's best-known melodies. And what inspiration may he have drawn on for his work? Anyone who has witnessed the sun rising over the composer's adopted home town of Garmisch-Partenkirchen will know at once, for art and nature are as one in Bavaria.

Albrecht Dürer (1471–1528)
Painter, graphic artist and art scholar, left the most varied body of work in German art. The Nuremberg-based artist was one of the first living north of the Alps to examine Italian Renaissance art, its achievements finding expression most clearly in his copper engravings and woodcuts. Here we see a self-portrait at the age of 28.

Walther von der Vogelweide (c. 1170–1230)
The ballads collected around 1330 in the *Weingartner Liederhandschrift* display the work of the most famous medieval German poet, Walther von der Vogelweide. The great lyric poet's songs have lost nothing of their fascination. This master of the high *minne*, or courtly lovesong, probably found his final resting place in Würzburg.

10. Jahrgang — Preis 20 Pfg. — Nummer 16

SIMPLICISSIMUS

Illustrierte Wochenschrift

Abonnement vierteljährlich 2 Mk. 25 Pfg. — Billige Ausgabe — Bayr. Post-Zeitungsliste: No. 834 — Billige Ausgabe

(Alle Rechte vorbehalten)

Der Brite (Zeichnung von Wilhelm Schulz)

Der schürt die Zwietracht, wo es geht,
Und blüh vergnüglich in die Glut;
Brennt's in Europa sicherlich, so sieht
Sein Roß von Feuer. Ihm ist wohl zu Mut.

Simplicissimus

First published in 1896 by Albert Langen (1869–1909), *Simplicissimus* was a weekly forum for the literary avant-garde and an outlet for criticism of prevailing conditions. Among its regular contributors of drawings and articles were contemporary Munich artists such as Olaf Gulbransson (1873–1958), Frank Wedekind (1864–1918) and Ludwig Thoma (1867–1921).

Oskar Maria Graf (1894–1967)

Heinrich Mann described him as a "stroke of luck for Germany's opposition," while Rainer Maria Rilke praised his artistic corpus. The writer Oskar Maria Graf saw himself as a Bavarian popular poet. After the National Socialists took power, Oskar Maria Graf emigrated to Vienna and later New York, where he is said to have always gone out wearing his *lederhose*.

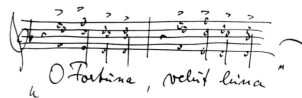

Carl Orff (1895–1982)

Since its premiere in 1937, Munich-born Carl Orff's Latin choral work *Carmina Burana* has enjoyed unbroken success. But Orff achieved worldwide celebrity not only as a composer, his Approach to Music and Dance Education becoming a lasting influence on the teaching of music to children the world over.

Gabriele Münter (1877–1962)

Jawlensky and Werefkin, 1909 (left). The artist couples Wassily Kandinsky and Gabriele Münter together with Alexej Jawlensky and Marianne von Werefkin took their inspiration from the Alpine landscape around their Murnau homes. As members of the *Blauer Reiter* (Blue Rider) group of artists, they created a new style of expressive painting and unique works of worldwide renown.

Lucas Cranach (1472–1553)

Born in the Upper Franconian town of Kronach, Lucas Cranach the Elder was one of the most important German painters and graphic artists of the Renaissance. The picture shows Katharina von Bora, whose marriage to Martin Luther he was a witness to. Over a period of five decades, Cranach filled his atelier with thousands of paintings, drawings, woodcuts and copper engravings.

Asam brothers

The huge fresco on the ceiling of the Asam Church in Ingolstadt is the work of the Upper Bavarian fresco painter and architect, Cosmas Damian Asam (1686–1739). The painting's central theme is the *Incarnatio Dominica*, the incarnation of the Son of God. Cosmas frequently collaborated with his brother, the plasterer and sculptor Egid Quirin Asam (1692–1750). Their combined talents raised the Asam brothers to their status as leading exponents of German rococo.

Richard Strauss (1864–1949)

Born in Munich, Richard Strauss wrote his first pieces at the age of six. The composer and conductor achieved worldwide renown mainly by virtue of his operas. Strauss died at his home in Garmisch in 1949. Here we see the original score for Richard Strauss' fanfare, composed for the occasion of the Viennese Philharmonic's 1st ball on 4 March 1924.

141

How a little boy of Turkish parentage grew into
a true Lower Bavarian.

"Django was always one of us."

When the two of them meet up, the air is alight with Lower Bavarian wit and charm. Facing one another are one of Germany's best-known cabaret artistes and the director of the House of Bavarian History. Uğur Bağışlayıcı, alias Django Asül, and Dr. Richard Loibl grew up as neighbours in the market town of Hengersberg in the shadow of the Bavarian Forest. "The moment you stuck your head out of the door, you saw Uğur come racing round the corner on his wheelie bike," recalls Richard Loibl with a smile. "My formative years were spent among Lower Bavarian aborigines like you. What good fortune!" comes the riposte from Django Asül in perfect dialect.

The Bağışlayıcı couple moved to Bavaria in 1970, with Uğur being born a couple of years later. As both his parents worked factory shifts, little Django-to-be spent a lot of time at their neighbours'. "My playpen was the whole neighbourhood. I was made welcome everywhere." He was often served his dinner at friends', and one family even gave him a room of his own and took him along on holiday with them. "All the women round about loved Uğur," grins Richard Loibl. "You were always hearing what a good little boy he was. It got on my nerves sometimes, especially when they'd just caught you fishing where you weren't allowed to." Uğur wasn't one to get up to mischief. "Him, he was always interested in everything, particularly the way people spoke. What's that called? Why do you say it like that?" And the little boy drank in not only the dialect he heard. "Emotionally, I'm 90 per cent Lower Bavarian, too." These days, the cabaret performer incorporates both Bavarian and Turkish stock characters into his routines. There was always plenty of material just waiting to be given a taste of his sharp wit. On Sundays, for example, his neighbour always used to take him along to sit at the regulars' table at the pub. "Craftsmen, freelancers, insurance brokers, bank employees. They were all there, and I always sat plum in the middle."

"Richard, your mum always had a bit of sausagemeat for me. Even back then, I knew this place was where I felt truly happiest. I was never going to leave." To this day, Django Asül (right) lives in Hengersberg, and is always pleased to see his boyhood pal, Richard Loibl. "Hengersberg really is a bit special. And we've all made something of our lives."

Juergen Teller is one of the most influential and
style-setting photographers in the world.

"Perfection bores me."

He dumped Kate Moss on a wheelbarrow and stuffed Victoria Beckham
into a shopping bag. He is the only photographer to have been allowed
to photograph Charlotte Rampling as nature created her – and that while
in the Louvre, too! His pictures of Kurt Cobain, Elton John and Björk are
also world-famous. Juergen Teller has had just about everybody in front
of his lens, all our contemporary icons, in arresting, self-ironic poses,
often bare-faced and unbeautified, affable and natural. He describes the
essence of his work as follows – "The only thing that really interests me
is the interaction between two people. One of those people is me, the
photographer. And when an encounter moves me, then it's going to be
good." Juergen Teller has revolutionized fashion photography, because
he doesn't place his subject in a scene of perfection, but rather tries to
find their human side. In the words of Paul Klee, "Art does not repro-
duce the visible; rather, it makes visible."

It may be that this particular way of presenting people has something
to do with his origins. Juergen Teller grew up in a family of violinmak-
ers in the Middle Franconian community of Bubenreuth. A dust allergy
prevented him from carrying on the family tradition, and led him to
veer from the prescribed path. He studied from 1984 to 1986 at the Bavarian State Academy of Photography in Munich, before moving to London.
His breakthrough came with the pictures he took of Sinéad O'Connor
for the cover of her worldwide hit, "Nothing compares to U." This led to
a stream of photographs appearing in magazines like *Vogue* and *The Face*.

Today, the artist's work is in demand everywhere from London
to New York and Sydney, but this globetrotter has never forgotten his
home country. "For me, Bavaria is the place I come from." Many of his
artworks are noticeably autobiographical, dealing with his family and
origins. His favourite place, he says, is "the woods between Bergkirchweih
in Erlangen and our house in Bubenreuth. Woods like those are called
steckerleswald, which are monocultural pine forests. As a child, I played
there nearly every day, and today, I like to use the woods for my work,
as a photographic subject or as somewhere to stroll." A wonderful oath
of allegiance from an atypical man to something so typically Bavarian,
a man who is at once deeply rooted in his native town and still broad-
minded – just like Bavarians altogether.

Be it Kurt Cobain (bottom) or Kate
Moss (opposite page), some of the
best-known images of these icons
were created by Franconian Juergen
Teller (top), who has himself become a worldwide star. He still likes
to return to his home country. Teller
has been Visiting Professor of Photography at Nuremberg's Academy
of Fine Arts since 2014.

A matter of opinion!

"Bavaria is my home when I'm in Europe. When I think of Bavaria, I immediately see the cleanliness, the cosiness, its location right in the centre of Europe, the best airport in the world. Great audiences, packed concert halls."

Al Di Meola (b. 1954),
American musician and one of the most famous jazz guitarists in the world

---

"The quietness in Bavaria is something you don't easily find in China. On the way to Neuschwanstein Castle, my German friend, who was driving, kept proudly telling me to look at the beautiful scenery of Bavarian suburbs and finally found me asleep. For me it's too much green, maybe."

Bert Chi,
China

"They were an unwashed sort, unbathed and nonetheless more receptive to art than their scrubbed brethren in the North."

Theodor Lessing (1872–1933),
German philosopher

"My ancestors come from Lower Bavaria. My father moved to neighbouring Baden-Wuerttemberg as a young man and was unhappy all his life, far from home, and he was more than pleased when his son then moved back to Bavaria. Characteristic of Bavaria is its sense of being close to the soil, and the straightforward way people are with each other. That's just their temperament."

Professor Gerhard Ertl (b. 1936),
German scientist and honorary professor at Munich's Technical University; winner of many awards, including the Nobel Prize for Chemistry

---

"All southern Germans are much, much nicer than we are, and the nicest are the Bavarians, because they are the most natural."

Theodor Fontane (1819–1898),
German writer

"I think the best thing about Bavarians is their irrepressible hedonism: Bavaria's glorious cuisine, its delicious beer and the really cosy atmosphere when they celebrate something!" *

"Munich society sets great store by its traditional grumpiness. Challenge a grumbler to cheer up and they'll just do the opposite and grumble all the more. I personally see grumbling as an important way of smoothing out the day's little irregularities, otherwise I'd have to pretend everything was fine. There's always something you can grumble about – the weather, or your sales figures, or people come past who think they can let off steam at us BISS paper sellers. At heart, I'm actually perfectly happy, but I like a nice grumble every now and then."

Wolfgang Urban,
who sells a street magazine like *The Big Issue* in Munich

"Bayern is inspiring – the interplay of town and country, the traditional and the modern, nature and culture is a major factor. Differences are honoured and enjoy equal status. The Bavarian is a relaxed individual, close to nature and open-minded. *"Pack ma's wieda"* ("Let's go for it") is a Bavarian saying full of pragmatism, self-confidence and solidarity.

Dr. Christine Bortenlänger (b. 1966),
Head of the Munich Stock Exchange for many years and Chief Executive of the DAI, Germany's Institute for Share Promotion

* Commentary on the Facebook fanpage "Unser Bayern" www.facebook.com/bayern

"It's typical to love your Bavarian home country and feel proud of it, even when you're not running around in *lederhose* trousers or a *dirndl* dress. Traditional costume is Bavarian, but not those Oktoberfest *dirndls* and floppy felt hats. Being Bavarian is an affair of the heart, not a choice of clothing."*

———————

"There's nowhere you can come across more torturers, scallywags and henchmen than in Bavaria."

Wilhelm Ludwig Wekherlin (1739–1792),
German journalist

———————

"My wife, Sabine, comes from Bavaria. We met as students in Paris and now live in Tokyo. My staff work very hard. They would never leave the office before me, and, of course, sometimes I stay on a bit longer. But when the work is done, I head for home. That's why I tell my staff how important one particular word is to my wife. It's *'feierabend,'* hometime. If I'm not home at a decent hour, I've apparently not been working efficiently, she says. So, if the work's done, there's no reason to do any overtime."

Emmanuel Thierry,
French accountant

"The Bavarian landscape is an experience and very varied. We've got everything from urban to rural, lakes to mountains, and we enjoy it ;-) What we can't deny is that we are rather stubborn, but great lovers of our heritage."

Anna Schaffelhuber (b. 1993),
monoskier; competed in five races at the 2014 Sochi Paralympics and won five gold medals; winner of many awards, including the Bavarian Sports Prize

———————

"Bavaria is just something you feel."*

———————

"What I like best about Bavaria? Its deep cultural fabric, sensibility towards quality, its sense of family values and, of course, *weißwurst*. Normally, I was never much of a consumer of beer, but my first taste of Franziskaner changed my relationship to this beverage forever."

Kent Nagano (b. 1951),
Californian-born conductor, acknowledged as an outstanding opera and orchestra conductor, general director of music at Munich's Bavarian State Opera from 2006 to 2013

"Bavaria is not just a Free State, it's a state of being."*

———————

"It's a tribal attitude to resist outside ideas for a good while but then to accept them and bring them to fruition."

Professor Benno Hubensteiner (1924–1985),
Bavarian historian

———————

"The typical Bavarian is warm-hearted, friendly, fun-loving and makes for a great friend."*

———————

"I think, just once in a while, we can say that God would feel at home in Bavaria."

Alfred Kerr (1867–1948),
German writer and theatre critic

Bavarians on the move

Around five million people in the Free State regularly do sport,
whether in clubs, with friends or on their own. Certain sports are a permanent
feature of Bavaria's culture.

Skiing and snowboarding – even in summer!

No problem on Monte Kaolino in Hirschau in the Upper Palatinate. The 'white mountain' is actually a 35-million-ton hill of quartz sand accumulated as a by-product of decades of quarrying kaolin, used to make porcelain. The sand sports elite gather at Monte Kaolino for their European and world championships. The Bavarian Alps provide fine conditions for winter sports.

Schafkopf is trumps!

Munich's Schafkopf School calculates that there are 99 561 092 450 391 000 variations of the card game Schafkopf ('Sheep's head'), all of which require cleverness, combining skills and tactical awareness. It is played with 32 cards, four players and – at least in its 'pure' form – in accordance with rules drawn up in the Upper Palatinate town of Amberg in 1895. Up and down the land, Bavarians attend tournaments to play their national card game.

Ran an die daubn! (Hit the stave)

Bavarians enjoy their winter sports, too. Out they go onto the frozen ponds and lakes to try and propel a wooden curling stone as near as possible to a little wooden stave-shaped target. In many villages, the members of the local shooting club compete against each other. A new trend has brought special spotlighted curling lanes to beer gardens.

Martial arts Bavarian-style

In Bavaria, they like to put each other over a barrel, using one finger and in accordance with strict rules. Finger-wrestling involves two opponents facing each other across a table, slipping a middle finger into a leather ring and waiting for the word, "Both wrestlers ready? Show us!" Then they pull for all they're worth. The winner has to yank their opponent over to their side of the table, which usually happens within seconds. It is said that, at one time, disputes were settled in this fashion. Today, finger-wrestling is an organized sport with Bavarian, German, Austrian and Alpine championships every year.

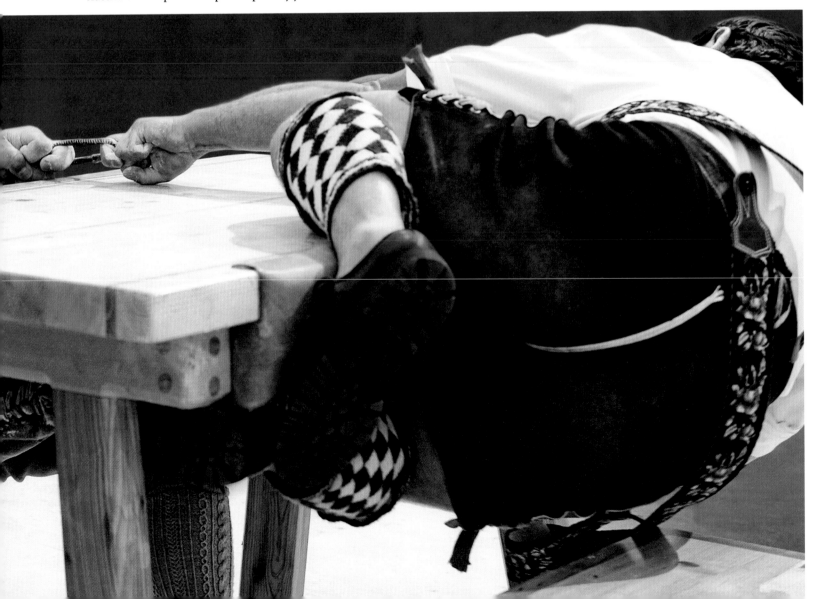

Kassandra Wedel is Europe's only deaf dance instructor –
and hip-hop world champion.

"I feel the beat in my belly!"

Thirteen dancers stand poised in the mirrored studio at the
Munich GSC School of Dance. The music starts, and they begin to
dance. Effortlessly, they adapt their hip-hop moves to the rhythm.
Kassandra Wedel demonstrates each element to her students.
Music and movement dissolve fascinatingly into one another – and
leave onlookers astounded. For how can anyone dance so wonderfully – without being able to hear the music?

   Kassandra lost her hearing as a result of a car accident at
the age of three. Seven of her students are also deaf. "I feel the
rhythm with my whole body. That doesn't mean the music has
to be loud, as long as it's got a good bass to set the room vibrat-
ing." The deaf 30-year old has been teaching deaf and hearing
people hip-hop for the last ten years. Her inclusive dance troupe
call themselves 'Nikita.' The Munich teacher gives instructions
using sign language, and the spoken word for those who are not
conversant.

   In 2001, the passionate hip-hop dancer became German for-
mation-dancing champion as the only non-hearing member of her
group. She and her group Nikita have also won awards at inclusive
championships where people with normal hearing dance together with deaf people. They were German hip-hop champions
in 2012, also being runners-up at the world championships the
same year. "I've been dancing since I could walk. Dancing is my life.
It gives me freedom and self-confidence." And it helps to over-
come prejudices. "A lot of people don't think deaf people can dance
or do a whole lot of other things. That's why I formed Nikita,
because dance is like music – it unites us all."

Teaching in sign language – a class
with Kassandra Wedel. She formed
her inclusive group in 2004 at
the age of 19, and was Europe's first
professionally-qualified deaf hip-
hop instructor. And Kassandra
is not only a pace-setter as a dancer –
she is also Germany's only deaf
theatre studies graduate.

The perfect wave

He is a legend among big-wave surfers, those professional surfers who go out looking for the biggest waves in the world. In 2010, Sebastian Steudtner was the first European to win Hawaii's surfing 'Oscar' by riding what was at the time the world's biggest wave – a 72-foot-high giant. A big wave can weigh anything up to 500 000 tons and race towards the coast at speeds of up to 50 mph. The Franconian feels at home on these waves the size of houses. His goal is to locate the world's biggest wave (and suspects it may be found in Europe) and to regain the world record, which currently stands at nearly 80 foot. Steudtner moved to Hawaii in 2001 at the age of 16 with the intention of becoming a professional surfer. He discovered his love of the water on the lakes and rivers of his home town of Nuremberg.

> "Who cares about all that junk? We're world champions, we've got the cup, you can shove your golden boot up your jersey."

When asked about failing to win the Golden Boot awarded to the top goalscorer at the World Cup.

> "I reckon he knows who I am now."

Of Diego Maradona after Germany's 4-0 quarter-final win over Argentina at the 2010 FIFA World Cup. Before the tournament, Argentina's coach had referred to him as a ballboy. Müller went on to be the tournament's top scorer.

Multiple German league championship and cupwinner, winner of the Champions League, the World Club Championship and world champion – Thomas Müller, born in 1989, has won just about everything there is to win in football. As a boy, he played for TSV Pähl before making it into Bayern Munich's D youth team at the age of 11. He is still at the club.

The Bavarian who loves to '*müller*'

"And there he is. Thomas Müller shuffles over with a wide smile and a warm *servus*. In five seasons as a first-team footballer, he has won two doubles and a treble with Bayern, and one World Cup with Germany. He still doesn't move, talk or look like a top international footballer, and he still couldn't care less about that observation. That's his secret. All that success has done is make him even more comfortable in his good-natured *naturbursche* (nature boy) skin. This is the Bavarian idea of 'cool.' (...) His exploits have created their own verb. *Müllern*, to *müller*, aptly describes his clever, unashamedly inelegant art of stabbing the ball home from unlikely angles with unlikely parts of his head or legs."

This was how one British reporter raved in the *Guardian* about Thomas Müller. And how right he was! Nobody magicks up goals – or witty remarks – like this Upper Bavarian.

Printed by kind permission of Guardian News & Media Ltd

"Mario Götze, how does
it feel to win the league wearing
the right colours?"

To his teammate Mario Götze,
who had been transferred to Bayern Munich
from Borussia Dortmund.

———————

"I'm gradually getting the
feeling my left foot's
good for a bit more than just
heading for the pub."

During the FIFA 2014 Wold Cup.

———————

"If you've got no muscles,
there's nothing to get hurt.
My legs are so thin,
the other player can't even see
the bone he wants to kick."

On the fact that he has had
so few injuries.

Well, look at that!

Jimi Hendrix first smashed a guitar on stage at the trendy Big Apple club in the Munich suburb of Schwabing. It was 9 November 1966. The still-unknown performer had accidentally broken his guitar and, in a fit of rage, smashed it to pieces right there on stage. The gesture became his trademark at appearances around the world.

For 600 years, the Upper Palatinate town of Windischeschenbach has been producing a special brand of beer called **Zoigl** (a dialect form of the word *'zeichen,'* meaning 'sign'). Thirty-eight of the townspeople run a communal brewery. A year in advance, they decide which of them will be given the brewing licence. The beer is then fermented in the homebrewer's cellar and served up in home pubs – *'zoiglstuben.'* A six-pointed sign representing water, fire, air, malted barley, hops and yeast, is hoisted outside whichever house is currently serving.

In 1266, the wife of the mayor of Deggendorf in Lower Bavaria repelled a spy by flinging **dumplings** at him. The enemy fled, later reporting to his master, the army leader Ottokar of Bohemia, that the people of Deggendorf had so much to eat that they could afford to throw it around. At which point the siege was called off.

In 1966, the Augsburg footballer Helmut Haller scored the opening goal for Germany in the legendary World Cup final at Wembley. Germany went on to lose the match 4–2 to England, but Haller grabbed the match ball and smuggled it out of stadium. Thirty years on, a British newspaper collected 80 000 pounds to buy the **Wembley ball** from Haller. The ball is now on display at the National Football Museum in Manchester.

"When you live in Berlin, you drink *Club Mate*," they say in the capital. Berlin's 'in' drink, a carbonated and caffeinated mate tea concoction, is produced in Münchsteinach in Middle Franconia.

The International Astronomical Union named an asteroid after the Franconian scholar, **Simon Marius** (1573–1624). The astronomer from Gunzenhausen in Middle Franconia discovered Jupiter's four major moons at almost the same time as Galileo.

Bavarian is regularly voted Germany's most erotic dialect. Aw, get off!

In November 1885, Chicago rushed for tickets to see a touring theatre company. Every performance at the Lincoln Theatre and the Grand Opera House was sold out. The company in question was the folk comedy ensemble, *Schlierseer Bauerntheater*, performing 'Haberfeldtreiben' (Court of Reproval) and 'Jägerblut' (Blood of the Hunter) in German.

All a-buzz. While stars emerge from the wings at the Munich State Opera House, 200 000 bees are busy producing honey on the roof of the National Theatre. The National Theatre shop offers *'Opernhonig'* (opera honey) at the start of the festival season.

157

The Free State

"I love this state, the oldest
and most established of all
the German states and one
of the oldest in Europe. I owe
it much and I expect even
more from it."

Werner Bergengruen (1892–1964),
German-Baltic author

Afternoon view
from the Walhalla
over the Danube.

Blue and white or white and blue?

Guests and newcomers are generally soon convinced that the Bavarians are peace-loving and agreeable. Irritation arises – if it does at all – when they rhapsodize not only about Bavaria but also about its "blue-and-white" state colours, only to be sharply corrected straight away: "That's white-and-blue, just so you know."

The rebuke has nothing to do with a busybody's platitudes but rather with the fact that this presumably trivial lapse cuts to the chase, so to speak. There are a few subjects on which a Bavarian has no choice but to speak up – otherwise it will tear him apart. This includes 'Ruhpòlding' with the accent on the second syllable, which the Bavarian tends to counter with a bouncy dactylic 'Rùhpolding,' or the name 'Karl Valentin,' pronounced with an English V, which inevitably entails a "That's Valentin – with a V as in 'fish!'"

But in the case of Bavarian white and blue, let's turn first to the highest authority. The constitution of the Free State of Bavaria stipulates in article 1, paragraph 2: "The colours of the land are white and blue." This is consistent with two places in the Bavarian anthem, which has been dignified by nothing less than an official statement by the Minister President. Its first verse ends: "…and keep the colours of His heaven, our white and blue." And the end of the second verse concludes: "…and may that glory be preserved by our Banner, white and blue!"

Thus three times the official sequence of white and blue, and it goes without saying that we also see this reflected in semi-official texts. These would include, above all, the comedian Weiß Ferdl, who, in his song about the Bavarian banner, pledges himself almost eulogistically to this colour doctrine: "Right in the middle the Danube flows through, hollerä hollaridulio, / And our banner is white and blue." It has been claimed that it is primarily for poetical reasons that the sequence white-blue has become so popular: 'blue' is simply a better rhyme word than 'white.' This is debatable. Weiß Ferdl could surely also have versified differently: "And up in the North, live the Prussians all right, hollerä hollaridulio, / But our banner wafts blue and white".

Seen scientifically, the plea that God keep the colours of his heavens white and blue is difficult to justify, since – from the day of Creation – the Bavarian sky has been blue-white: white clouds on a blue background. And speaking of white: Are you familiar with the Austrian war flag? A white eagle on a white background. Very funny, but we Bavarians are allowed to say this as a reprisal for Austria's theft of the region south-east of the Inn River in 1779.

But from the sky back to the earth, or, more precisely, to the counts of Bogen, who have had the white-blue lozenges, or *fusils,* in their coat of arms since 1204. When Count Albert IV died childless in 1242, his stepbrother Duke Otto II of Bavaria succeeded him; in order to document the new possession, he also adopted the lozenges of Bogen and in this way made them into the Wittelsbach, that is to say, the Bavarian coat of arms. The lozenge escutcheon has survived through the centuries in different versions and today can be seen in the state coat of arms in the form of an inescutcheon surrounded by a golden lion, a blue panther, the 'Franconian rake' and the three black lions. Without these henchmen, but with the *volkskrone* ('people's crown') above, it is also used as the "small state coat of arms."

But now for the main point, and, in this, the historian and heraldry expert Wilhelm Volkert serves as our authority. For the sequence, he says, what is decisive is the colour found in the upper left-hand corner of the escutcheon – left as seen by the viewer, that is, though in the heraldic sense right. This fluctuated somewhat very early on, but, from the early 16th century, the priority of the colour white in the upper left prevailed in official illustrations, and, with this, the sequence of the colours was resolved.

One final little point: The *Brockhaus* encyclopedia of 1887 shows the coats of arms of the most important civilized states on a double-page spread. Number one: the Kingdom of Bavaria.   *Hermann Unterstöger*

Hermann Unterstöger
Hermann Unterstöger has been writing for the *Süddeutsche Zeitung* newspaper for three and a half decades. He became known for his reports on page three and the humorously didactic column *'Streiflicht.'* As the head of the *'Streiflicht'* team, he accepted the Henri Nannen Award in 2005. For his writing style, the Upper Bavarian was awarded the Ben Witter and Ernst Hoferichter prizes; during the awards ceremony it was said, "Unterstöger's texts represent their own kind of form, something between journalism and art."

Ayzit Bostan
Fashion designer, artist and design professor – born in 1968 in Ankara, Ayzit Bostan arrived in Munich at the age of four, and still lives and works there today. The design on the right-hand page is called *'Wolke'* ('Cloud') and dates from 2014.

In the beginning was Napoleon

The French emperor triumphantly entered Munich on 26 October 1805. Shortly beforehand, the Electorate of Bavaria had shifted its allegiance to the French. As a result, Bavaria gained a royal crown, a greatly-enlarged territory and its first liberal constitution. This was the birth of modern Bavaria – and its 'midwife' was Napoleon. The more urbanized and industrialized new Bavarian regions of Swabia and Franconia were now combined with the less urban, overwhelmingly agrarian and Catholic Old Bavaria. It was now necessary to bridge the religious and economic differences through extensive reforms. Present-day Bavaria's cultural diversity is based above all on the success of this integration.

Bavaria – The Constitutional State

During the Napoleonic Wars, Bavaria – cleverly manoeuvring between hostile camps – retained its independence and thus ensured the survival of its kingdom, which was a truly heterogeneous complex of 'Old Bavarians' on the one hand and Swabians and Franconians on the other. The first kings attempted to elicit, rather than force, a common identity. The cement that was used for this consisted of loyalty to the royal house and to the Bavarian constitution of 1818.

The constitution established the constitutional monarchy, with the *Landtag* (state parliament) to represent the people. Suffrage was limited to the upper and middle classes, but there was suffrage and there was a constitution to which the king felt bound. The Great Powers of the German Confederation, Prussia and Austria, achieved this only after the March Revolution of 1848. The Bavarian kings – and this is truly sensational – did not have themselves crowned, but rather took oaths upon the constitution. By doing so, they did not place themselves above the state, but aligned themselves within it.

In this way, the politics of consensus, liberality and proportional representation – typical of Bavaria – was established. Include as many as possible, weigh the regions equally, balance out the interests, progress in moderation, preferably combined with tradition.

Bavaria was in favour of modifying the constitution only gradually, which was sometimes too slowly. But the Bavarians were nonetheless able to achieve a federalist design to the imperial constitution of 1871. But, in 1919, they failed miserably: the Weimar Constitution was democratic but centralist. The new Bavarian constitution came too late; imperial law overrode state law.

In 1945, the Bavarians had learned from this experience. A two-pronged approach was needed, one that emphasized the Bavarian more than the German, if possible. The Bavarian constitution was adopted by plebiscite, in contrast to the Basic Law of 1949, which was voted upon

On 26 May 1818, Maximilian I Joseph 'bestowed' a constitution upon his people. The constitution, which was very progressive and liberal for the time, was also meant, not least, as an offer to the newly acquired regions. A Franconian citizen made the following comment: "It is … now a great pleasure to belong to Bavaria. … It is only with this constitution that our king has conquered Ansbach and Bayreuth, Würzburg, Bamberg and the others."

Anlage.

Verfassungsurkunde des Freistaates Bayern.

Das bayerische Volk hat durch den am 12. Januar und 2. Februar 1919 gewählten Landtag dem Freistaate Bayern diese Verfassung gegeben:

1. Abschnitt.
Staat, Staatsgebiet, Staatsgewalt.

§ 1.

I Bayern ist ein Freistaat und Mitglied des Deutschen Reiches. Die bisherigen Landesteile Bayerns in ihrem Gesamtbestande bilden das Staatsgebiet.
II Die Landesfarben sind weiß und blau.

§ 2.

Die Staatsgewalt geht von der Gesamtheit des Volkes aus. Sie wird nach den Bestimmungen dieser Verfassung und der Verfassung des Deutschen Reiches unmittelbar durch die Staatsbürger und mittelbar durch die in dieser Verfassung eingesetzten Organe ausgeübt.

§ 3.

I Dem Landtage steht die Ausübung aller Rechte der Staatsgewalt zu, die nicht durch diese Verfassung oder die Verfassung des Deutschen Reiches der Staatsbürgerschaft, den Behörden oder den Verbänden der Selbstverwaltung vorbehalten sind.
II Die dem Landtage zustehenden Rechte und Aufgaben sind unübertragbar, soweit diese Verfassung nichts anderes vorsieht.

§ 4.

Das Gesamtministerium ist die oberste vollziehende und leitende Behörde des Staates. Es wird von dem Landtage bestellt und ist diesem verantwortlich.

§ 5.

Die Rechtspflege wird durch unabhängige, nur den Gesetzen unterworfene Gerichte ausgeübt. Die Gerichte sind Staatsgerichte. Ihre Einrichtung erfolgt durch Gesetz.

2. Abschnitt.
Staatsbürgerschaft.

§ 6.

Staatsbürger ist ohne Unterschied der Geburt, des Geschlechtes, des Glaubens und des Berufes jeder Angehörige des bayerischen Staates, welcher das zwanzigste Lebensjahr vollendet hat.

§ 7.

Der Staatsbürger übt sein Bürgerrecht aus durch Abstimmung
1. bei Volksanträgen und Volksentscheidungen,
2. bei Wahlen.

§ 8.

Jeder Staatsbürger hat das Recht, an den durch diese Verfassung vorgesehenen Abstimmungen und Wahlen teilzunehmen, wenn er seit mindestens sechs Monaten seinen Wohnsitz in Bayern hat. Das Stimm- und Wahlrecht wird, soweit nicht durch Gesetz Ausnahmen zugelassen sind, am Wohnsitz ausgeübt.

§ 9.

Von der Ausübung des Stimm- und Wahlrechtes ist ausgeschlossen:
1. wer entmündigt, unter vorläufige Vormundschaft oder wegen geistigen Gebrechens unter Pflegschaft gestellt ist,
2. wer infolge strafgerichtlicher Verurteilung die bürgerlichen Ehrenrechte nicht besitzt.

§ 10.

I Volksanträge können nur gerichtet werden:
1. auf Abänderung der Verfassung,
2. auf Erlaß, Abänderung und Aufhebung von Gesetzen, soweit solche nicht von der Volksentscheidung ausgenommen sind (§ 77 Abs. I),
3. auf Einberufung oder Auflösung des Landtages (§ 30).
II Volksanträge sind an den Landtag und, wenn dieser nicht versammelt ist, an das Gesamtministerium zu richten. Sie sind vorbehaltlich der Vorschriften des § 30 Abs. I und IV rechtswirksam bei einfachen Gesetzen, wenn sie von mindestens einem Zehntel, bei Verfassungsgesetzen, wenn sie von mindestens einem Fünftel der Staatsbürgerschaft gestellt werden.
III Volksentscheidung findet nur in den von dieser Verfassung vorgesehenen Fällen statt. Sie ist rechtswirksam bei einfachen Gesetzen, wenn mindestens ein Fünftel, bei Verfassungsgesetzen, wenn mindestens zwei Fünftel der stimmberechtigten Staatsbürger daran teilgenommen haben. Vorbehaltlich der Vorschrift des § 30 Abs. IV entscheidet einfache Mehrheit, bei Verfassungsänderungen Zweidrittelmehrheit der abgegebenen gültigen Stimmen. Die Abstimmung ist allgemein, gleich, unmittelbar und geheim. Sie kann nur bejahend oder verneinend sein.
IV Das Verfahren bei Volksanträgen und Volksentscheidungen wird durch Gesetz geregelt.

§ 11.

I Jeder Staatsbürger hat in der Gemeinde seines Wohnsitzes das Gemeindebürgerrecht. Er kann es nur ausüben, wenn er seit mindestens sechs Monaten im Gemeindebezirke wohnt.
II Die Ausübung des Wahlrechtes in den Gemeinden darf nicht von der Entrichtung einer Gebühr abhängig gemacht werden.
III Die Regelung der besonderen Rechte und Pflichten aus dem Gemeindeverbande bleibt der Gesetzgebung vorbehalten.

Napoleon's star went down – but the achievements remained through the constitutional work of the "all-powerful minister" Maximilian von Montgelas. In Bavaria, people were in favour of continuing to develop this accomplishment gradually. And, after all, a federalist design was achieved with the imperial constitution of 1871. But in 1919, they failed miserably; the Weimar Constitution was democratic but at the same time centralist.

after the parliamentary council in Bonn only by the *Landtage* (state parliaments) of the eleven western states. On 1 December 1946 – concurrently with the first *Landtag* election after the war – 70 per cent of the electorate decided in favour.

The Basic Law of the Federal Republic was, in essence, prepared at the Munich Conference of Minister Presidents of 1947, initiated by Bavaria, and at the Herrenchiemsee constitutional conference of 1948. Bavaria had a right to be satisfied with the Basic Law, which took effect in 1949, even if, for many people, it did not go far enough with respect to federalist elements. The phrasing, "No to the Basic Law and Yes to Germany," enabled the representatives to be both in favour and against at the same time – yet another Bavarian idiosyncrasy of value in the future.   *Dr. Richard Loibl*

Bavaria from the revolution to the end of the National Socialist dictatorship

"Suddenly, behind us two shots ring out, one after the other, Eisner staggers a moment, tries to speak but his tongue fails him. Then he silently collapses. It all happened in a fraction of a second."

This is an eyewitness account of the murder of Minister President Kurt Eisner, a fatal turning-point in Bavarian history. And everything had begun so deceptively peacefully. The plea attributed to Oskar Maria Graf – "Let's make a revolution today, so that there's peace and quiet!" – has often been quoted. The monarchy of the Wittelsbachs had outlived its usefulness, a new beginning was sought, preferably calmly. Kurt Eisner was its initiator. He came from Berlin, from a Jewish family, and was a journalist, social democrat and the leader of the breakaway USPD party, and, not least, a Bavarian patriot. During the great peace demonstration on Munich's Theresienwiese on 7 November 1918, he pressed the anti-revolution majority social democrats into the background and, with the help of the soldiers, accomplished a bloodless coup. From now on, Bavaria was to be a Free State, in which the Bavarian people were meant to enjoy "the freest self-determination."

After the lost war, it was clear to Eisner that only a radical transition to a democratic society could save the future. He saw the old elites as unfit to achieve this. Seen from a present-day perspective, he was right. But at the time, he was alone with his opinion. His clear confession of Germany's war guilt cost him a great deal of sympathy in a militarized society. In Bavaria, he was not even helped by his enthusiasm for federalism. For the Berliner, Bavaria was a hotbed of liberal, democratic and social traditions. The new 'United States of Germany' was to be formed from the South outwards and no longer by Prussia. But the path Eisner recommended to achieve this, a new state treaty between the German states together with Austria, was rejected even by the southern German states.

After a smear campaign from both the right and left, Eisner and his USPD lost the *Landtag* (state parliament) elections in 1919. Women were allowed to vote for the first time; in addition to the introduction of the plebiscite and the 8-hour workday, this was one of Eisner's important reforms. On the way to the *Landtag,* where he planned to announce his resignation, the Minister President was assassinated on 21 February 1919, after only 100 days in office.

This bloody act had the worst possible repercussions. The Communists, whom Eisner had held in check, called for a new revolution. The Bavarian government fled to Bamberg and called upon the Bavarian people to join together into a corps of volunteer military units ('freikorps') and free Munich. Later, imperial troops arrived as support. There were

The end of the war came as a complete surprise to many people, because the government had misled them until the very end with announcements of victories. The legend that the revolutionaries around Kurt Eisner (1867–1919) had "stabbed the heroes from the front" in the back had disastrous consequences.

> ## "Let's make a revolution today, so that there's peace and quiet!"
>
> Oskar Maria Graf (1894–1967)

The beginning and end of the Free State of Bavaria in the Weimar Republic – the demonstration on the Theresienwiese on 7 November 1918 marked the birth of the Free State of Bavaria. On 9 March 1933, the National Socialists stripped the Bavarian Minister President, Heinrich Held, of governmental power.

Deutſche Reichspoſt

480 BLITZ BERLIN 40 + 84/82 9/3 2015

aus

	Aufgenommen					Befördert	
Tag	Monat	Jahr	Zeit	= MINISTEPRAESIDENT DR HELD	Tag		Zeit
09	III. 33	20--	45	MUENCHEN =			
von		durch			an		durch
Berlin 1				7023			
Amt München				PCD =			

DA DIE INFOLGE UMGESTALTUNG POLITISCHER VERHAELTNISSE IN DEUTSCHLAND HERVORGERUFENE BEUNRUHIGUNG IN BEVOELKERUNG OEFFENTLICHE SICHERHEIT UND ORDNUNG IN BAYERN GEGENWAERTIG NICHT MEHR GEWAEHRLEISTET ERSCHEINEN LAESST , UEBERNEHME FUER REICHSREGIERUNG GEMAESS PARAGRAPH 2 VERORDNUNG ZUM SCHUTZE VON VOLK UND STAAT BEFUGNISSE OBERSTER LANDESBEHOERDEN BAYERNS SOWEIT ZUR ERHALTUNG OEFFENTLICHER SICHERHEIT UND ORDNUNG NOTWENDIG UND UEBERTRAGE WAHRNEHMUNG DIESER BEFUGNISSE GENERALLEUTNANT RITTER VON EPP IN MUENCHEN . ERSUCHE DIESEM SOFORT GESCHAEFTE ZU UEBERGEBEN .

(11./32)

skirmishes, and shootings of hostages and prisoners. The revolts were crushed at the beginning of May 1919. But their repercussions continued. The people had become more radicalized and armed. The *freikorps* also fostered the rise of right-wing extremists. Added to this was widespread disappointment with the centralistic Weimar constitution. In this climate, fuelled by the currency crisis and hyperinflation, Hitler's rise to power took place. On 8th and 9th November 1923, at the Munich Bürgerbräu beer hall, he called for a march on Berlin and, together with Ludendorff, placed himself at its head. At the Feldherrnhalle, the Bavarian police put a quick end to the terrible episode, but the justice system gave Hitler not only a forum during his trial in 1924 but also a very light sentence and the best confinement conditions in Landsberg Prison.

Its prohibition in 1923 naturally created problems for the NSDAP. The economy was picking up appreciably. A degree of prosperity was drawing support from the radicals of both the left and the right. In Bavaria in the 1920s, a structural shift took place and more people were now employed in industry than in agriculture. The NSDAP seemed no longer to represent a danger. In 1925, the prohibition against it was lifted. In the *Landtag* elections of 1928, it got only six per cent. But then came the Great Depression of 1929. When unemployment almost doubled in Bavaria shortly thereafter, NSDAP support multipled. In the elections of 1932 – the last free ones – the incumbent Bavarian Peoples Party (BVP) and the NSDAP ran neck and neck; the BVP won in the end with only three tenths of a percentage point lead. The NSDAP had poor results in the majority Catholic regions of Lower Franconia, Swabia, the Upper Palatinate, Upper and Lower Bavaria after the Catholic Church had threatened party members with excommunication.

At first, until the middle of March 1933, Bavaria held its ground against the National Socialist seizure of power. But then, here too, they took over governmental authority. Bavaria seemed initially to profit economically from the Nazi regime: in 1934 – the construction of the Munich-Salzburg autobahn was begun in Unterhaching in 1936. Hitler opened the IV Winter Olympic Games at the ski stadium in Garmisch-Partenkirchen. Hitler focused special attention on Munich, which was distinguished with honorary titles such as 'The Capital of the Movement.' No other German city in the provinces was given so many prestigious and administrative buildings, such as the 'Haus der Deutschen Kunst,' opened in 1937. Nuremberg, formerly a stronghold of the SPD party, was transformed into the city of the Nazi Party rallies (*reichsparteitage*) with a gigantomaniac project. Until 1942, Hitler himself spent almost half his time in Obersalzberg.

Around six million European Jews were murdered in the Holocaust. Women, men and children were victims of the Nazi extermination mania – including in the Free State. The Nazi regime laid the foundation for its reign of terror from the very beginning. Opposition politicians in Bavaria were driven into exile, imprisoned or murdered. Only a few days after the Nazis seized power, the concentration camp in Dachau was opened – an especially chilling monument to Nazi terror: originally intended for political opponents of all camps, the 'model camp' and training centre for the SS stood for repression, torture and murder. In 1935, the anti-Semitic Nuremberg Laws were proclaimed. And in 1938, *Kristallnacht* took place in Bavaria as well, with terrible acts of violence and without any resistance to speak of against the persecution of Jewish fellow citizens. From 1941 onwards, many were deported to the extermination camps in the east.

The mood towards the regime began to change only after the war started, especially when the bomb war reached Bavaria. Liberation came, and National Socialism's reign of terror ended in the spring of 1945. Most of Bavaria was allocated to the American occupation zone and thus was given the best conceivable starting position for the future.   *Dr. Richard Loibl*

'Bread and Circuses' – the National Socialists were masters of propaganda nomenclature. The reign of terror celebrated itself at the Nazi Party Rallies in Nuremberg. The Winter Games of 1936 in Garmisch-Partenkirchen were meant to deceive the public abroad (left page).

Everyone who rejected the regime or who did not fit into the 'people's community' was ruthlessly segregated and persecuted. In Bavaria, one of the first German concentration camps was built in Dachau (top). In the end, many Bavarian cities lay in ruins. In Würzburg, more than four-fifths of the city was destroyed.

A White Rose for freedom

28 April 1945: many Munich residents are taken aback when they turn on the radio in the morning. None of the usual Nazi rallying calls. Instead, they hear an appeal to offer no resistance to the advancing US troops and to 'take care of' the Nazi functionaries. What had happened? The 'Bavarian Freedom Initiative,' led by Munich officers around Rupprecht Gerngross, had occupied two radio stations. Almost 1000 citizens in 78 Bavarian towns took part in the initiative, in order to end the senseless fighting against the Allies. The SS violently foiled the initiative. Two days later, Munich was liberated by the Americans, not by its own people. But the people of Munich memorialized the courageous attempt by renaming Feilitzschplatz 'Münchner Freiheit.'

"Nothing is so unworthy of a civilized people as allowing itself to be 'governed' without opposition by an irresponsible government clique that has yielded to base instinct." Words from the first pamphlet of the 'White Rose.' Under this name, a group of students around Hans and Sophie Scholl, Alexander Schmorell, Christoph Probst and Willi Graf assailed the Nazi regime in 1942/43 with pamphlets and graffiti. They were also joined by philosophy professor Kurt Huber. Very few people stood up against Nazi injustice. The majority of the population succumbed to National Socialist ideas. Even among those who were critical, passivity prevailed.

One reason for this was certainly the relentless persecution of the Nazis' opponents by the Gestapo and the *Volksgerichtshof*, or 'People's Court.' Like the members of the 'White Rose,' many active resistance fighters paid for their courage with their lives, such as Munich's Georg Elser, a would-be assassin of Hitler, and Claus Graf Schenk von Stauffenberg, the leading initiator of an attempted coup on 20 July 1944.

What remains of the resistance fighters? The historian Golo Mann wrote in 1958: "If there had been … no one else in the German resistance other than the Scholl siblings and their friends, they alone would have sufficed to salvage something of the honour of those humans who speak the German language."

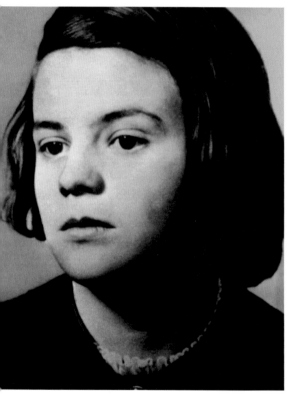

Sophie Scholl and her brother Hans were executed on 22 February 1943. Monuments in front of the Bavarian State Chancellery and at the Ludwig-Maximilians-Universität recall their heroic courage. Their legacy still lives on today. Franz J. Müller (right), member of 'The White Rose' resistance movement, founded the White Rose Foundation in 1987.

9 November 2013 – FC Bayern Munich
fans commemorate the victims of the
Kristallnacht in 1938.

"Down with Hitler," "Hitler mass
murderer," "Freedom": the White Rose
fought the Nazi regime with graffiti
and pamphlets.

Dr. Jack Terry is spokesman for the former prisoners of Flossenbürg concentration camp. The 84-year-old gives the police cadets in Sulzbach-Rosenberg the following piece of advice: "Become good police officers under an independent system of law in your democracy. The memorial gave us back our human dignity. Today, I have good friends in Germany."

Dr. Jack Terry survived the concentration camp and works against forgetting.

"Flossenbürg has never left me."

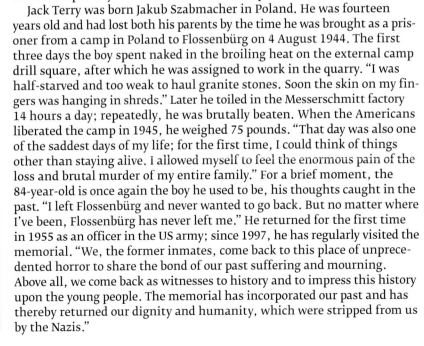

Dressed in running shoes and a t-shirt, Jack Terry stands in front of a group of young officers from Sulzbach-Rosenberg's riot police. "At first, we scarcely dared applaud. But he immediately put us at ease. It's unbelievable what a buoyant, strong person Dr. Terry is," marvels one of the cadets. "Especially after all the horror he's experienced."

Jack Terry was born Jakub Szabmacher in Poland. He was fourteen years old and had lost both his parents by the time he was brought as a prisoner from a camp in Poland to Flossenbürg on 4 August 1944. The first three days the boy spent naked in the broiling heat on the external camp drill square, after which he was assigned to work in the quarry. "I was half-starved and too weak to haul granite stones. Soon the skin on my fingers was hanging in shreds." Later he toiled in the Messerschmitt factory 14 hours a day; repeatedly, he was brutally beaten. When the Americans liberated the camp in 1945, he weighed 75 pounds. "That day was also one of the saddest days of my life; for the first time, I could think of things other than staying alive. I allowed myself to feel the enormous pain of the loss and brutal murder of my entire family." For a brief moment, the 84-year-old is once again the boy he used to be, his thoughts caught in the past. "I left Flossenbürg and never wanted to go back. But no matter where I've been, Flossenbürg has never left me." He returned for the first time in 1955 as an officer in the US army; since 1997, he has regularly visited the memorial. "We, the former inmates, come back to this place of unprecedented horror to share the bond of our past suffering and mourning. Above all, we come back as witnesses to history and to impress this history upon the young people. The memorial has incorporated our past and has thereby returned our dignity and humanity, which were stripped from us by the Nazis."

After the war, the Tannbach River served as the demarcation line between Soviet-occupied and American-occupied zones in Mödlareuth. From 1966, an impregnable cement wall dissected the village. Since 1989, an unobstructed view of the landscape is once again possible (from upper left to lower right).

'Little Berlin' and the Bavarian doors to freedom

The 9th of December 1989 is a cold and gloomy winter day in Mödlareuth. But to the village's residents, the weather doesn't matter – they embrace each other jubilantly. In the icy temperatures, the people are celebrating a historic moment with Bavarian beer and Thuringian bratwurst: the end of the division of their village. One month after the fall of the Berlin Wall, the concrete wall that had mercilessly bisected this village on the border between Bavaria and Thuringia had also fallen. "The happiest people on earth" – today, this describes the people of Mödlareuth.

The Americans called this divided town, 'little Berlin.' After the end of the Second World War, the victorious powers divided this village along the Tannbach River: the western part, which had from time immemorial been part of Upper Franconia, went to the Americans. The eastern part, which was part of Thuringia, came under Soviet occupation. Whereas visits between the two were possible in the beginning, starting in 1952 East Germany unilaterally extended its border installations. Barbed wire, spring guns and concrete now separated families, friends and neighbours – for 37 long years.

The consequences of the division shaped life for entire regions: around 500 miles of iron curtain hung between Bavaria and the Eastern Bloc. The town of Hof no longer lay at the heart of Europe but rather in the 'zonal border area.' Anyone living in the shadow of the wall felt the division up close – but also the good fortune freedom and democracy signified.

There was great joy when, in 1989, Hungary was the first country to open its borders to the West. The refugees from the GDR who then fled across the border were greeted with a wave of helpfulness. Volunteer helpers built tent camps, distributed food, gave out welcome money. Almost 45000 people fled the GDR through the Bavarian doors to freedom.

With the fall of the Wall and reunification in peace and freedom, a divided country has become a united Germany once again. Today the 'Deutsch-Deutsches Museum' in Mödlareuth reminds visitors of the message of our history: justice, freedom and democracy are not to be taken for granted, but are the ongoing task of every generation.

Wall and boundary posts, formerly instruments of the division of Germany, today remind visitors to the open-air museum in Mödlareuth that freedom and democracy cannot be taken for granted. An entire village out and about: on 9 December 1989 the Wall fell in Mödlareuth. Families, neighbours and friends from East and West celebrate their long-awaited reunion and seal the end of their village's division.

DEUTSCHE DEMOKRATISCHE REPUBLIK

With his epistolary novel about the parliamentary representative 'Jozef Filser,' author Ludwig Thoma created a true Bavarian cult figure. Bottom: the staircase and colonnades of the Maximilianeum, seat of the Bavarian *Landtag* (state parliament) since 1949.

A royal pain!
Who's in charge in Bavaria?

"The surest proof that Bavaria is the terrestrial paradise of Germany lies in the fact that this province ... has up to now been capable of enduring a government that is generally recognized as the worst among all the terrible governments in Europe."

There's no question – these words from 1796 are entirely historical! They come from the *Ansbacher Mémoire* of Maximilian Graf von Montgelas, superminister to King Maximilian I and architect of the modern Bavarian state. He is responsible for the system of qualified civil service, the administrative regions and obligatory schooling in Bavaria, among other things.

Today, Bavaria is a Free State with elected representatives of the people. "The profession of a parliamentarian is gruelling and one makes great sacrifices for the constituency" – still today, many a Bavarian member of parliament might agree with this cri de coeur from 'Jozef Filser,' the parliamentary representative in Ludwig Thoma's famous epistolary novel.

Bavaria is proud of its autonomy. Bavaria's voice carries special weight both in Germany and abroad. Not only for this reason do many consider the office of Bavarian Minister President the best job in the world. It is accompanied by unusual privileges. For example, every year, the Bavarian Minister President is given the first *'maß'* of beer when the keg is tapped at the Oktoberfest's opening ceremony.

Several Bavarian Minister Presidents began as local politicians. In Bavaria, the mayors, county councillors and district assembly presidents have a strong position in the constitutional structure. They shape policy with the people locally – all state authority springs from the people. That is the Bavarian attitude to life!

A view of the nerve centre of democracy – deputies attending a policy statement by Minister President Seehofer on 12 November 2013; Seehofer congratulates Barbara Stamm on her re-election as state parliament president on 2 October 2013; Visitors to the state parliament on Open Day 2014 (clockwise from top).

The Free State

Fritz Schäffer
1945

Dr. Wilhelm Hoegner
1945–1946 and 1954–1957

Dr. Hans Ehard
1946–1954 and 1960–1962

Bavarian Minister Presidents since 1945

"The Bavarian people have something anarchical about them. For this reason, the art of governing here has always consisted of making the unpredictable predictable."

Die Welt newspaper, 19 January 2007

Dr. h.c. Alfons Goppel
1962–1978

Dr. h.c. Franz Josef Strauß
1978–1988

Dr. Hanns Seidel
1957–1960

Dr. Edmund Stoiber
1993–2007

Dr. Günther Beckstein
2007–2008

Dr. h.c. Max Streibl
1988–1993

Horst Seehofer, since 2008

Horst Seehofer was born in Ingolstadt on 4 July 1949. In 1970, he completed his university of applied sciences degree as a public administration specialist. He worked in the administrative district offices in Ingolstadt and Eichstätt until 1980. In 1980, he became a Bundestag representative for the electoral district of Ingolstadt, staying until 2008. In 1989, Seehofer became parliamentary state secretary to the federal minister for employment and social security, in 1992, federal minister for health. He was a member of the Merkel cabinet from 2005 to 2008 as federal minister of food, agriculture and consumer protection. From 1994 to 2008, Seehofer was deputy party leader of the CSU and has been party leader since October 2008. On 27 October 2008, the Bavarian *Landtag* (state parliament) elected Horst Seehofer Bavarian Minister President and confirmed him in office on 8 October 2013. From November 2011 to October 2012, Horst Seehofer was president of the German *Bundesrat* (Germany's federal chamber). Since October 2013, he has been *Landtag* representative for the electoral district of Neuburg-Schrobenhausen. Horst Seehofer is married and the father of four children.

Bavaria's representative offices

Bavaria has representative
offices in
Brazil (São Paulo)
Bulgaria (Sofia)
Chile* (Santiago de Chile)
China (Shenzhen und Qingdao)
India (Bangalore)
Israel (Herzliya)
Japan (Tokyo)
Canada (Montréal)
Croatia (Zagreb)
Mexico (Mexico City)
Austria (Vienna)
Poland (Warsaw)
Romania (Bucharest)
Russia (Moscow)
Switzerland (Zurich)
South Africa (Johannesburg)
Czech Republic (Prague)
Turkey (Istanbul)
Ukraine (Kiev)
Hungary (Budapest)
USA (New York and San Francisco)
United Arab Emirates
(Abu Dhabi)
Vietnam (Ho Chi Minh City)

*Also responsible for
Argentina (Buenos Aires)
Colombia (Bogotá)
Peru (Lima)

At home abroad

12 Michalská Street, a grand building in the heart of Prague, has been housing Bavaria's representation in the Czech Republic since 2014. A 29th-floor view across the St. Lawrence River is afforded by the Free State's representative office in Montréal/Québec. The Institut Pasteur in Brussels' Parc Léopold is home to Bavaria's representation in the midst of the European quarter (p. 182, top). Staff at a total of 25 Bavarian representative offices abroad are busy spinning an international web of contacts for the Free State. It is their daily business to assist Bavarian firms entering the world's major markets and to persuade foreign enterprises to locate to Bavaria. 'Foreign policy' is only natural for Bavaria. Which is why Bavaria also has representative offices at 21–22 Behrenstraße, just along from the Brandenburg Gate in Berlin.

A chief task of the missions is to bring Bavarian companies to the attention of national and European policymakers. Whenever political decisions are made – be they by the federal government, in Germany's Bundestag or its Senate, Bavarian politicians are always involved. Bavaria also makes its voice clearly heard in Brussels, where EU laws are shaped. These missions also act as a forum for information-gathering and exchanges of views. Politicians, diplomats and journalists can meet and talk with major decision-makers. The 'white-and-blue embassies' are popular meeting-places in the cultural and political life of Berlin and Brussels.

The white-and-blue flag has long been a trademark recognized far beyond Europe's borders. The Free State is held in high esteem around the world. How else could Bavaria consort with such high-calibre partners? Why do heads of national governments and world powers seek to cooperate with the Free State?

Answer number one – the Free State is not just any state in Germany or elsewhere. Bavaria can look back on more than a thousand years of history. Its people

The Bavarian delegation on
Behrenstraße, in the heart of
the government quarter, was
opened in 1998. It was the first
state delegation in Berlin.

A meeting of friends – Bavarian state Parliament President Barbara Stamm welcomes Bulgarian State President Rosen Plevneliev to a working discussion at the Bavarian *Landtag* on 30 January 2014. Bavaria is well connected, even far beyond the borders of Europe. Following a joint meeting in Beijing on 24 November 2014, Bavarian Minister President Horst Seehofer (left) presents the Premier of the People's Republic of China, Li Keqiang, with a jersey from football club FC Bayern Munich. Eight is considered a lucky number in China.

foster a very particular perception of 'State,' not least as a consequence of the kingdom it called into being over 200 years ago.

Answer number two – Bavaria is highly-respected the world over as a trading partner, an engine of innovation and a vanguard of the megatrends of the future. Bavaria is unique in Germany in hosting over 100 foreign consular missions.

Answer number three – the future belongs to those regions which are strong. The very best compete with each other. The leading regions seek to cooperate and learn from one another. This is why Bavaria has created the 'Power Regions' group: biennial summits take place between Bavaria's Minister President and the government leaders of Québec, Upper Austria, Shandong, the Western Cape, Georgia and São Paulo – all of them Bavaria's strong partners spanning four continents. These high-level meetings lead to numerous joint projects, whether in research and technology or in education, the arts and culture.

Answer number four – Bavaria is the state at Europe's heart. Bavaria has for centuries been the bridge between east and west, north and south. Bavaria radiates its assets as a business location and cultural nation in all directions. The Free State makes no distinction between love of one's home country and receptivity to all things new. It is this attitude to life on which the Bavarians draw to shape their future.

Bavaria's home in Prague – the Bavarian representative office is housed in the Palais Chotek, which places it in the heart of Prague's Old City, and symbolizes the friendship that has developed between Bavaria and the Czech Republic.

Well, look at that!

Bavaria is the state with the **lowest unemployment** in Germany. The rate in May 2014 lay at 3.6 per cent (to compare: Berlin, 11.1 per cent; Germany as a whole, 6.6 per cent).

According to the Jacobites, **Franz, Duke of Bavaria**, the head of the House of Wittelsbach, is, as successor to the Stuarts, the legitimate king of England, Scotland, Ireland and France.

Bavaria bears over half the burden of the **inter-state fiscal equalization scheme.** The Free State currently has to pay 4.3 billion euros. From 1989 to 2013, Bayern has thus paid a price-adjusted 50.9 billion euros towards inter-state fiscal equalization and thus several times the amount it has received in roughly forty years (since 1950, price-adjusted, around 9.8 billion euros).

Anyone who marries a Bavarian becomes a Bavarian oneself – and that's according to the Bavarian constitution (article 6: **Citizenship by marriage**).

Bavaria is the **safest state** in Germany. In 2013, 5 073 crimes were committed per 100 000 inhabitants; in Munich, 7 395; the average in Germany as a whole is 7 404; in Berlin, 14 908 and Frankfurt am Main 16 292.

She was described as the "only man in the *Landtag*" – during Hitler's putsch on 9 November 1923, **Ellen Ammann** (1870–1932) was the first to inform the Bavarian state government, organized the resistance and obtained the car that brought the Bavarian politicians from the danger zone of Munich to the safety of Regensburg. The fact that Hitler was unsuccessful in 1923 is largely due to her.

Highest fiscal policy rating:
The credit rating agency Moody's attested to a "clever and prudent budget management, low public debt, debt reduction, budget surpluses in the course of recent years and an exceptionally strong and diversified economy" in the Free State in 2014.

Laptop and *lederhose*:
The famous quotation by retired Federal President Roman Herzog, born in Lower Bavaria, describes the special combination of tradition and modernity in the Free State.

The future

"Bavaria has the genetic make-up to reinvent itself."

Professor Wolfgang Ullrich (b. 1967), Bavarian art historian

The BMW Welt in Munich – BMW's new-car delivery centre is an architectural masterpiece.

unbeatable fuel efficie

Airbus Franz Josef Strauß was one of the fathers and sponsors of Europe's largest aircraft construction company. Technological advances made in Bavaria have contributed a regular impetus.
Linde Munich's Linde AG provided the central element for Europe's largest natural gas liquefaction plant in Hammerfest, Norway.

Global Player

The Airbus 330 banks gently. Finally coming in to land in Vancouver after a ten-hour flight. The engine noise changes pitch as the Pacific bathes in the glow of the setting sun. Off into the wild tomorrow! Along the route to the hotel – a sign with the letters MTU. A Bavarian enterprise at Vancouver airport.

MTU Aero Engines has a staff of around 9000 at locations in Germany, Poland, China and the USA as well as in Canada. Its HQ, however, is in Munich. Beginning life in 1913 as the Rapp Aircraft Engine Works, switching in 1971 to building turbines for civil aircraft, before today producing the most eco-friendly of engines for the A 320 neo, MTU's progress is a perfect example of the industrial history of Bavaria.

Bavarian roots and global success are characteristic of numerous global players located in Bavaria. BMW's and Audi's premium vehicles are coveted products on every continent. Across the world, MAN's trucks, buses and turbomachinery help to move people and goods. From their bases in the little Middle Franconian town of Herzo-genaurach, Adidas and Puma have become global brands loved by sports enthusiasts the world over. The world is insured by Allianz and Munich Re. Siemens, Infineon and Linde lead the world in shaping our high-tech future.

The combination of superb infrastructure and outstanding specialists in a research-intensive environment make the Free State an ideal region to locate to. It's no wonder that international combines choose to set up shop in Bavaria – prime examples are Google and Microsoft in Munich and the Swiss pharmaceuticals giant Roche in Penzberg. General Electric built its European research centre in Garching. Come to Bavaria to take a look at the future.

Siemens Siemens' Velaro is one of the world's fastest high-speed trains currently in operation.
Puma Puma developed the Theseus II golden running shoe for world sprint champion Usain Bolt.

SIEMENS

Adidas Happy in Adidas – artist Pharrell Williams designed a special collection for Europe's largest sports goods manufacturer.

Allianz Munich-based Allianz is one of the world's largest insurance groups.
Münchner Rück Munich Re is the world's largest reinsurer. One of Germany's biggest-ever insurance losses came after 1986's 'hailstorm of the century.' (Here, a reconstruction of the biggest hailstone)
MAN MAN's trucks and buses enjoy worldwide renown by virtue of their technical perfection and advanced automotive technology. (Here, a six-cylinder engine)

Three individuals with a common goal

The future doesn't just happen. It is shaped. By individuals going down unknown paths, thinking differently and eager to make things happen. Entrepreneurs, scientists and researchers in Bavaria all share a common goal – displaying courage, stamina and creativity, they are all working towards developments which will improve all our lives. Below are just three of the many thinkers and doers in Bavaria.

Dr. Reinhard Janta, board member at Carbon Composites e. V. (CCeV) and long-serving site manager of SGL Group in Meitingen
While it is, physically, a lightweight product, carbon fibre has a massive presence. Car and aircraft parts are made of his company's carbon-fibre-reinforced plastic. "Carbon fibres are far lighter than steel or aluminium," Reinhard Janta enthuses, "but still extremely stable." Less weight means electric cars have a greater range. The lighter an aircraft is, the farther it can fly on the same quantity of fuel. That cuts costs and protects the environment. But other challenges remain. "Carbon fibres are yet to become mass-production articles." Swabia is an area supporting development – a unique carbon fibres knowledge cluster has grown up around Augsburg. "Together, we are working on automating production processes and reducing production costs."

Susanne Lang, managing director of Mekra Lang

82 years ago, Frieda and Hans Lang established a mirror manufactory. "My grandmother took care of the business side and my grandfather of all the technical issues." Susanne Lang has long been familiar with the idea of women executives, and, today, she heads the company based in the Lower Franconian town of Ergersheim which produces eight million wing mirrors a year for commercial vehicles. Mekra Lang is the world leader in its field and specializes in making the blind spot visible. And nothing important about running the company escapes the eye of the boss either. "To make a company grow, you have to help the staff you've got." They have an on-site kindergarten ensuring their workers' children are being well looked after. This Montessori service is available from 5:30 am to 6 pm, and on Saturdays if need be. There's even a production line conveyor belt especially for mums with small children who can only work shorter shifts. Just a few of the schemes which motivate staff – and make a major contribution to the firm's success.

Dr. Johannes Bange, cancer researcher

Johannes Bange has declared war on cancer. For years, the chemist has been working on an agent which specifically attacks tumours. "A lot of medications cannot distinguish between healthy and malignant cells. Antibodies can." They have fewer side-effects than chemotherapy. The drug is currently being tested. When it comes onto the market, it may well improve cancer treatment enormously. It is no coincidence that Bange's company, U3 Pharma, is located on the Martinsried campus. This is where the Munich Ludwig-Maximilians-Universität institutes, the Max Planck Institutes for Biochemistry and Neurobiology and the Innovation and Start-Up Centre for Biotechnology, have networked their knowledge. "If you're in research, you won't find better conditions anywhere in Europe."

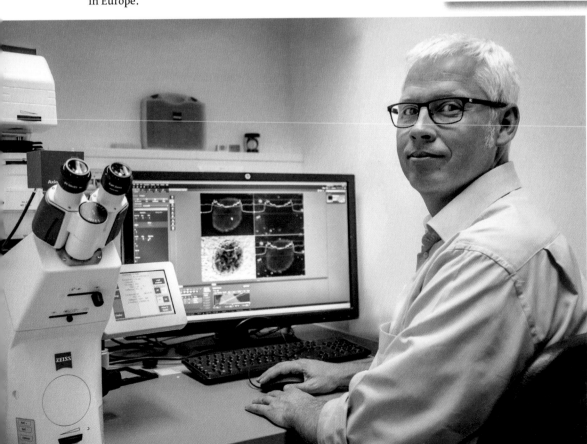

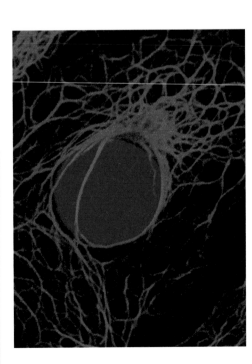

488 billion euros of economic clout

339
billion euros
was the turnover recorded in 2013 by manufacturing and processing firms in the Free State. Bavaria's industry is export-oriented and international, sending a record 52 per cent of its output abroad.

21
per cent more economic output
Bavaria's GDP rose more strongly between 2003 and 2013 than anywhere else in Germany. The national average was 13.7 per cent.

Around
18 800
firms
were founded in 2013, meaning Bavaria remains Germany's number one state for start-ups.

12
Munich-based listed companies
The state capital has been topping the national table of stock exchange-listed companies for years, according to a study by strategic consultants Simon-Kucher & Partners, not only in terms of the number of firms quoted but also as far as their stock market value is concerned. In May 2014, they were worth three times as much as their nearest rivals, Wolfsburg and Bonn.

16
crafts businesses for every
1000
inhabitants
illustrate how important the skilled crafts and trades sector is to Bavaria as a business location. Around one in three Bavarian apprentices is learning a craft.

156 000
more students
Between 1999/2000 and 2014/2015, the number of students in Bavaria climbed by 74 per cent from 211 000 to 367 000. University expansion since 2008 has created places for 50 000 new students.

As much as
3.6
per cent of GDP is to be spent on improving research and development
in Bavaria by 2020. A creative environment promotes innovation, product development and services, all vital to providing first-rate career opportunities and job security in the years ahead.

19
clusters
in key economic sectors are one result of Bavaria's Cluster Initiative aimed at networking research establishments and honing Bavaria's business competitiveness.

Unless otherwise stated, all figures refer to 2013.

3.6

billion
of prior debt will be paid off
by Bavaria between 2012 and 2016.
Bavaria has taken on no new
debt since 2006 and plans to be free
of all existing debts by 2030.

Around

40

million passengers
passed through Munich airport
in 2014. That means 380 000 take-
offs and landings, making
Franz Josef Strauss Airport one of
Europe's busiest air traffic hubs.
Particularly impressed by the typically Bavarian hospitality shown
by its staff, 12 million passengers
voted MUC the best airport
in Europe and the third-best in
the world in 2014.

At

25.8

per cent
industry's share of total Bavarian
output in 2013 was higher than in
any other part of the country.

---

1 114 000

**acres of sustainable natural
resources**
In 2012, about 1 114 000 acres of
land in Bavaria were given over to the
provision of renewable sources of
biogas, bio-fuels and their material
reutilization. That equates to
about 14 per cent of available arable
land. Energy producers in the
Free State currently use over 2 300 biogas plants covering 770 000 acres
to supply electricity to 1.6 million
households.

Over

5

million people
had jobs in the Free State in 2013
where they were liable for social security contributions – a historic high!

Over

26 000

**miles of state highways and
local trunk roads, including over
1 500 miles of motorways**
ensure every corner of the region
has ideal access to German
and European road networks.

226

million euros
in regional aid was disbursed
in Bavaria in 2013, primarily to spur
investment by small and medi-
um-sized enterprises, who were able
to hold on to 26 000 staff and create
jobs for 3 000 more.

---

14 829

patents
Bavaria is the land of tinkerers
and inventors. 14 829 patent applications came from Bavaria –
that's 31.3 per cent of the national
total, or 118 for every 100 000 residents. In Berlin, the figure was 27,
and 59 nationally.

Builders of the future

Neurochip implants, compostable nappies, underground pneumatic despatch systems – Nobel Prizewinner Theodor Hänsch is full of ideas. His mission is to improve our lives. He has assembled '100 products for the future,' solid proof of his creative spirit. As professor of experimental physics at Munich's Ludwig-Maximilians-Universität and director of the Max Planck Institute for Quantum Optics in Garching, Hänsch finds "that Germany is an excellent place for a scientist to work." Hänsch should know, having worked for many years in Stanford, California. Incidentally, one of his students there was Steve Jobs.

Bavaria is researcher country, with innovation and new ideas being supported by nine research-minded state universities and 17 state universities of applied sciences. The more artistically creative are drawn to the six state art colleges, including the renowned Munich University of Television and Film. Bavaria is host to highly-motivated top achievers, first-rate scientists and world-class researchers working at twelve Max Planck institutes, nine Fraunhofer applied research institutes, the Helmholtz Research Centre in Neuherberg, the German Aerospace Centre in Oberpfaffenhofen and Munich's Ifo economic research institute. Edvard Moser, winner of the Nobel Prize for medicine, did research at the Max Planck Institute in Martinsried. The elite wants to work with its own kind, arousing the interest of young students. Scientists and researchers inspire developers.

It's possible in Bavaria to see how ideas are turned into products. One example is the Fraunhofer Institute in Erlangen, where they have succeeded in developing high-speed camera systems capable of recording the otherwise invisible. Their high-speed camera takes up to 100 000 pictures per second, revealing processes that are normally too fast for the human eye. This 'fascination with the truly momentary' can be seen in film special effects, micro-motion studies in the field of medicine and crash tests in the car industry. Another forward-looking project attracting worldwide admiration is 5G, the ultra-fast data transfer technology

Combining the old and the new – the neoclassical Academy of Fine Arts in Munich was extended in 2005 to include a modern steel-and-glass construction. Around 120 million euros was invested in the top-to-bottom renovation of Augsburg University – the so-called KLM Building has housed the Faculty of Design since 2007.

The prizewinning Interim Main Lecture Hall (top) on the Garching campus of Munich's Technical University. Here, researchers from the Fraunhofer Institute for Reliability and Microintegration support firms developing robust electronics systems (bottom). The new building at Würzburg-Schweinfurt's University of Applied Sciences (below right).

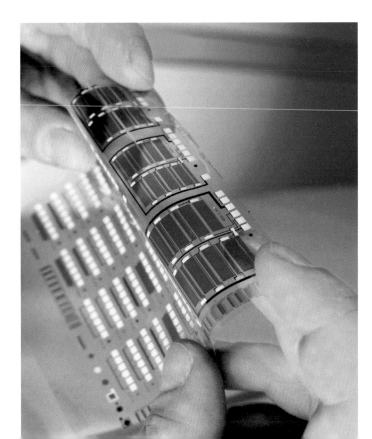

developed by scientists in Erlangen. In just a few years, it should be possible to download a full-length feature film in one second.

Bavaria has committed itself to key technologies with enormous growth potential, such as aerospace technology, ICT, life sciences, medical engineering, mechatronics, environmental engineering, material science and nanotechnology. 'Nano' is the Greek word for dwarf, but these dwarves can do amazing things. Nanoparticles, 50 000 times finer than the diameter of a human hair, make solar cells more efficient and rechargeable batteries longer-lasting, while the ultra-thinness of nano-coatings saves on natural resources.

From vision to implementation – Munich's 'House of Research' actively supports visionaries. Here, scientists and companies can learn what subsidies are available to help them make their breakthrough.

Ted Hänsch, as his friends call him, feels so at home in his Bavarian research paradise that he didn't want to retire. His protest was heard, and he now has a research job-for-life at LMU University – "as long as my health and strength are up to it."

The builders of the future are attracted to Bavaria, where, as the saying goes, "No time to count successes. Only the time ahead counts!"

Opposite: Extension to Bayreuth University (top); Straubing Scientific Centre (bottom). Right hand page: a scientist at Garching's Max Planck Plasma Physics Institute (left); Nuremberg Academy of Art (top); Munich University of Television and Film (bottom).

White, blue and multi-coloured – Bavaria is growing.

There has been a net increase in Bavaria's population since 1990 of 1.6 million people. 780 000 of these have come here from abroad, adding new colours to Bavaria's white-and-blue lifestyle. What brings people from every continent to Bavaria? What has surprised them? What has fostered their loyalty to the Free State?

Kenneth Walsh, born and brought up in Brisbane, Australia, bio- and chemical engineer
"My first visit to Bavaria was in 2009. With a girlfriend who loves Bavaria, a degree course which was best in Bavaria and a love of beer that can best be quenched in Bavaria, the decision to make this my home was an easy one. Bavaria unites the traditional and the modern – and that's how it should stay!"

Amir Roughani, Iranian-born graduate industrial engineer, named 2014 Entrepreneur of the Year by manager magazine
I was eleven when I first came to Berlin from Iran. I only moved to Munich after my degree. It wasn't long before I felt really at home in Bavaria. Here, unlike in Berlin, I have almost never felt like a foreigner. And anybody who lives in Munich or has ever spent time here knows it's one of the best places to have your home. That's why I founded VISPRON here in 2002, a tech firm now employing a staff of 400. Bavaria has become my second home, or, to quote the Bavarian TV slogan, 'I'm Amir, and I'm at home here.'"

Rahmée Wetterich, born in Cameroon, Africa, *dirndl* designer
"It's been nearly 36 years since my sister, Marie, and I came to live in Munich. Marie created the *dirndl à l'africaine*, a traditionally-cut *dirndl* using brightly-coloured African fabrics. Together, we created the Noh Nee fashion label. We want our creations to combine African and Bavarian culture so that people can see their own culture in an exciting new light. When I think of Bavaria, the first image that comes to mind is its white-and-blue sky – a bit tacky, I know, but always wonderful to come home to."

Adriana Ortega, born and brought up in El Paso, USA, working in international marketing and sales

I was born in El Paso. One day, I chanced to meet a group of Bavarians and immediately fell in love with their exotic language! That was ten years ago. I now live and work in the beautiful Allgäu region, my new home, where I play traditional Bavarian music. People always laugh when they find out that there's this Texan girl playing in the village chapel. But I can't think of anything more wonderful."

You Xie, born and raised in China, Bamberg city councillor, owner of a Chinese snack bar, prizewinning journalist and writer

"I came to Bamberg from Peking in 1988 to study journalism, German and law. I have learned a lot here, and I am still learning – about responsibility, liberty, solidarity, justice and tolerance. I have been a German citizen since 2010 – with all the privileges and duties which that entails. My motto is "Do not ask what your new home country can do for you. Ask rather what you can do for your new home country." The people here have made it easy for me to feel at home. Because I would like to give something back, I am involved in party politics. In 2014, I was at number 29 on the candidates' list for the city council, and the people of Bamberg voted me number one! That made me so proud!"

Celal Özcan, born and raised in Turkey, head of the Turkish newspaper, *Hürriyet Europe*

"When I arrived in Bavaria at the end of the Seventies, I was amazed at how similar Bavaria and Turkey were, almost as if they were related. The Bavarian saying, "We're us" sounds a bit less proud and self-confident than the exhortation ascribed to Atatürk, whereby "Lucky am I that I can call myself a Turk." And the Bavarian anthem can certainly match the Turkish one for pathos. People here also greet each other in the name of God '*Grüß Gott*' and '*Selam aleyküm.*' Bavaria's shoeslappers have an uncanny affinity with the Turkish zeybek, where men also leap into the air and slap the soles of their shoes. Nobody can say whether the Bavarians are descended from the Turks or the Turks from the Bavarians, but it can certainly be claimed that the Turks have integrated best in Bavaria. It just feels like home."

Claudien Hakizimana, born in Kenya, grew up in Hof, mentor for *Hofer Schulbegleitung*

"When I was four years old, my mother fled from the civil war in Rwanda with me and my three brothers. We were put up at a refugee hostel in Hof. The people in the town welcomed us warmly. My brothers and I have to thank our single mum for getting us successfully through grammar school – and Bettina Zschätzsch, from Hof. They always supported us and believed in us. Frau Zschätzsch formed the 'Hofer Schulbegleitung' project, whereby volunteer mentors assist children from disadvantaged families. And now it's me who can help others. I give swimming lessons and do tutoring. I'm just happy in Hof – and I'd like to give something back."

A darned clean economy!

Bavaria receives a lot of sun – and has a lot of people who take it and use it. A good 3 500 of them live in Furth, near Landshut, Germany's oldest solar community. The locals held their first solar energy day as far back as 1982. People came from near and far to inspect their photovoltaic systems. The community continues to be in the vanguard of developments. The people of Furth voted in 1999 to cover 100 per cent of their energy needs from renewable sources. Fifteen years later, they are up to 80 per cent – an example to communities across Europe. It brought them the 2014 German Sustainability Award, its sponsors pointing to how "Furth has managed to establish a culture of involvement which can carry the community into a sustainable future."

There are now people all over Bavaria getting involved in the dawn of a new age of energy, keen to ensure they have affordable and environmentally-responsible energy supplies without nuclear power. Saving energy, raising efficiency and generating more renewable energy – that's how we can preserve our resources.

The Free State leads in percentage of energy supplied by renewables. Bavaria is ahead of the rest of Germany when it comes to hydropower plants, biomass, geothermal energy and photovoltaics, and is pushing farther ahead with its new generation of solar cells. At the 'Solar Factory of the Future' at Nuremberg's Energy Campus, Franconian researchers are working to make solar cells cheaper and better, for example, with their printable organic photovoltaic modules. They have not only simplified the production process, but also cut power requirements and made new applications possible. The developments from Franconia mean it is now possible to integrate solar cells into house windows and smart-phone covers.

Subsidized by the Free State, the production companies involved are leading the way with their Green Factory Bavaria project. About 40 per cent of Bavarian electricity is consumed by industry, but now, various methods are available to achieve major energy savings. At Green Factory locations, enterprises can learn about energy efficiency. In Bayreuth, they can visit a complete energy-optimized production facility for parts made of carbon fibre-reinforced plastic (CFRP).

The combined heat and power plant on Würzburg's Friedensbrücke works in accordance with the environmentally-friendly cogeneration principle (left hand page). The Grünwald municipality focuses on geothermal energy (bottom).

Bavaria is a land of hydraulic power – the River Iller power station in Kempten is sustainable and modern. The Walchensee lake hydroelectric power station is recognizable by its six powerful penstocks (with Lake Kochel beyond). In Laufzorn, geothermally-heated water is drawn from 10 000 metre below the ground (top to bottom).

Green technologies are flourishing particularly well in Bavaria. There is a global demand for them, and the Bavarian economy exports nearly half its output.

There are fine examples throughout Bavaria, like the treatment plant in Swabia where the firm of Grünbeck is supplying clean water – to the people of Höchstädt but also customers in Haiti, Asia and Africa. Mainburg is home to another champion, where the heating engineers at the firm Wolf Heiztechnik lead Europe in the fields of climate control and ventilation technology. The Lower Bavarian company delivers tailor-made solutions, be they to detached homes with a high degree of energy self-sufficiency, Munich's Allianz Arena or a trade fair hotel in Abu Dhabi.

Bavaria is conscious of its responsibility to succeeding generations. We support the careful utilization of our resources and our energy. In the interests of our children and our grandchildren.

This farm has been in the family
for centuries, its beginnings traceable
as far back as 1300. Following a fire,
Hans Bürger-Schuster and his wife Kathi
have rebuilt their family business – and
protected themselves for the future.

Hans Bürger-Schuster heads a family-run farm
in Hof in Upper Bavaria.

The biogas plant generates 200 kilo-
watts of electricity, and there are
plans to raise its capacity. 13-year-old
Johannes hopes to take over the farm
from his father one day.

"Our warmth is a Catholic warmth."

Hans Bürger-Schuster still shudders when he recalls the night everything changed. "We had a technical defect in 2008 and our farm burnt down. Thank God no-one was hurt." The cost of the damage ran to 1 million euros. "We were unable to save half of our dairy cows or our harvest – a whole year's work went up in flames. And our home was suddenly transformed into a ruin." In their time of trouble, the couple and their three children received a lot of local help, and managed to rebuild the entire farm within four years – on a completely new basis. "These days, we are agriculturalists and energy farmers in one. Our photovoltaic and biogas plants supply our electricity, some of which goes to heat the parish church. So you could say, 'Our warmth is a Catholic warmth,' remarks Hans Bürger-Schuster with a grin – after his terrible ordeal, the master farmer can muster a smile again. Together with his wife Kathi and an apprentice, the 44-year-old works nearly 90 acres of modernized farmland. His 70 cows supply 400 gallons of milk a day. "I feel there's nothing better than working, together with my family, out in the open and with the animals." But his farm's produce benefits others, too. "I think we farmers are important for our region and for the land itself. We secure our food needs, and we cultivate and shape our landscape and nature. We are all working to preserve Creation for future generations."

"Who invented this?"
Bavarians at home and abroad!

1491–1494

The Earth flat? – not for **Martin Behaim**, a cloth merchant and mariner from Nuremberg. Between 1491 and 1494, he constructed his terrestrial globe, the '*Erdapfel*,' regarded as the earliest spherical representation of the Earth – even though the recently-discovered Americas were missing.

1655

Stephan Farfler, born in the Middle Franconian town of Altdorf in 1633, was a paraplegic. In order to get to church, he built himself a wheelchair vehicle featuring a manual crank and cogwheel transmission.

1790

David Heinrich Hoppe founded the Regensburg Botanical Society, today the world's oldest botanical association.

1797–1798

One of the greatest inventions in book-publishing can be credited to **Alois Senefelder** of Munich, who developed a process for reproducing pictures quickly and in any quantity. This was the birth of lithography, heralding the age of illustration.

1850

An engineer from the Bavarian heartland built the first submarine! In 1850, Dillingen-born **Wilhelm Bauer** constructed his '*Brandtaucher*,' or 'Wave-diver submarine apparatus,' the oldest submarine in the world still in existence. The '*Seeteufel*,' or 'Sea Devil,' followed in 1855. The Swabian's submersibles are regarded as the forerunners of our modern submarines.

1787–1826

A Lower Bavarian gave his name to the world-famous Fraunhofer Society – **Joseph von Fraunhofer**, from Straubing, who invented optical instruments and processes still useful today – without his research into light refraction, today's fibre-optic cables for data transfer might never have come about. The optician also produced high-quality lenses and telescopes essential to modern astronomy.

1873

Not to be put down – **Levi Strauss**, born in Buttenheim in Upper Franconia, created blue jeans as hard-wearing trousers for the gold-diggers in the Wild West. Now worn by the whole world.

1876

"Want a cold one? Linde's fridge will hold one!" **Carl von Linde** from Upper Franconia invented one of the most important household appliances of all – the refrigerator.

1855–1934

The Munich engineer **Oskar von Miller** built not only the Deutsches Museum for scientific exhibits but also Germany's first electric power station on Lake Walchensee – which was at the time the world's largest hydroelectric power station – which meant Bavaria was in 1924 the first non-city state in Germany to have a blanket electricity supply.

1882–1935

She was one of the most important scientists of the 20th century and the mother of modern algebra. Erlangen-born mathematician **Emmy Noether** made a significant contribution to putting her subject on a new footing and laying the foundations for modern-day information science.

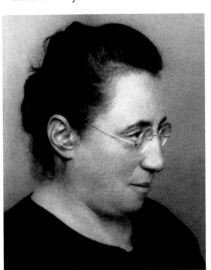

1895

Rudolf Diesel, the Paris-born son of an Augsburg craftsman and a craftsman's daughter from Nuremberg, invented an engine with very high efficiency. The diesel engine was ideal for moving heavy vehicles such as ships, tractors, trains, trucks and other machines.

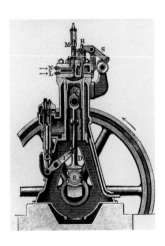

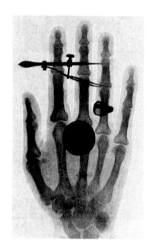

1903

The bicycle was becoming a method of transport for the masses – thanks in part to an invention by the Schweinfurt-based precision bearing manufacturers, **Fichtel & Sachs.** The first freewheel hub with an integrated coaster brake combined transmission, freewheeling and braking in one. Cycling at once became easier and safer.

Torpedo-
Freilaufnabe mit Rücktrittbremse.

1901–2002

He was one of the 20th century's most ingenious tinkerers – Rudolf Hell, born in Eggmühl in Upper Palatinate, was only 24 when he demonstrated his picture-scanning tube, making the invention of the television possible. Hell is also regarded as the father of the fax, the scanner and the news ticker.

1924

Better radio reception – engineer **Anton Kathrein** from Rosenheim put his economical and self-mountable wire aerial on sale. The Kathrein-Werke KG plant is today the world's oldest and largest aerial builder.

1951

Walter Linderer, from Munich, registered a patent for an 'appliance to protect vehicle users in collisions' – the forerunner of the airbag.

1952

The birth of the Barbie doll, who was originally named Lilli. The comic character first entertained readers of the *Bild* newspaper in 1952 with her long legs, blonde mane and cheeky remarks. Lilli soon came out as a doll, produced by Lower Franconian firm **Hausser.** The US company, Mattel, discovered the doll, bought the manufacturing rights from Hausser and launched Lilli onto the American market as Barbie.

1895

Light that gets under your skin – at Würzburg University, **Wilhelm Conrad Röntgen** discovered x-rays, which are known in German by his name. Six years later, his work earned him the first-ever Nobel Prize for Physics.

1971

Günter Schwan-häußer, from Lower Franconia and boss of the Middle Franconian firm Schwan-Stabilo, invented the highlighter for marking passages of text swiftly and easily.

1971/72

In the Middle Franconian town of Zirndorf, **Hans Beck** designed the first Playmobil figure. These figures can now be found in nurseries the world over.

1970

Karl Wald, a hairdresser and referee from Penzberg in Upper Bavaria, suggested to his football association that drawn matches should be decided after extra time by penalty shoot-out and not, as was the case until then, by the toss of a coin or drawing of lots. The regulation was introduced in Bavaria for the 1970–71 season. Shortly after, the German football association, the DFB, followed suit, and soon UEFA and FIFA likewise – much to the chagrin of many British footballers.

1987–1995

An invention from Erlangen in Middle Franconia revolutionized the music industry – a team at the Fraunhofer Institute under the leadership of Professors **Hans-Georg Musmann** and **Karlheinz Brandenburg** developed an algorithm for integrated circuits which for the first time allowed stereo music to be encoded in real time. Starting in 1995, the file format was called mp3, and enabled music to be compressed for storage and use on computers, the internet and mobile devices.

2008

In Munich, **Dr. Manfred Stefener's** team developed the first portable fuel cell, usable, for example, in electric vehicles and camper vans.

2009/10

Martin Aufmuth, a teacher from Erlangen in Middle Franconia, developed his One-Dollar Glasses, with a spring steel frame and ready-made, click-in plastic lenses. Their materials cost about a dollar, and it was Aufmuth's aim to enable people living on a dollar a day to afford glasses.

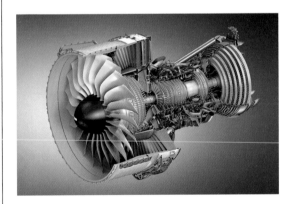

2013

Munich-based turbine manufacturers **MTU** developed an aircraft engine 50 per cent quieter and 15 per cent more fuel-efficient than its conventional rivals.

Secomba counts among Germany's most exciting start-ups. Their success is not a chance occurrence – "We work at weekends and on holiday, but we're working on our own product with people we ourselves have brought together."

Andrea Pfundmeier and Robert Freudenreich are making data on the internet secure.

"We turned down a seven-figure takeover offer."

From garage-door salesman to global combine – everyone is familiar with the success stories of the internet's pioneers. "Making something out of nothing? We can do that, too!" thought Andrea Pfundmeier and Robert Freudenreich. The commercial lawyer was just 23 and the information scientist 26 when they started up their firm, Secomba, in Augsburg in 2011. The two Swabians met at a university seminar for company founders and soon realized that, together, they were a dream team. "Robert had the idea, I had the commercial and legal background and both of us wanted to do our own thing." At the time, the information scientist was working on a program to digitalize student IDs. When he couldn't find any software to encode company data for storage in the cloud, the internet's databases, Freudenreich wrote his own program, Boxcryptor, and put it online. Within a week, the prototype had been downloaded over 1 000 times. "And we knew – this was the one!"

Their encryption software now runs on eight operating systems und twenty cloud providers – "No-one else has managed that." Downloads now total over 1 million. Even major combines and government agencies have bought licences. And there was even a takeover offer on the table from America – for a seven-figure sum. "We wanted to shape things ourselves, so we rejected it," recounts Robert Freudenreich coolly. His business partner adds, "This afternoon, we had a spontaneous outing with our staff to a beer garden. And I can bring my dog Caipi to the office if I want to. Such liberties are beyond price." And the Augsburg team plan to go on growing like this. The many prizes they have won – most recently, the 2014 German Initiative StartUp Award – point to the likelihood of their success.

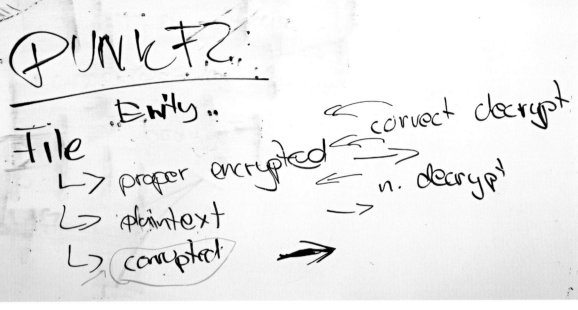

Many private users and firms turn to clouds like the dropbox. The growing need for internet security means sales of Boxcryptor are rising. The software allows data to be encrypted with just a few clicks.

Inventing has been on the school syllabus in Fürstenzell
in Lower Bavaria – for over 30 years.

"The best ideas come to us when we are pottering around together."

Christoph is nobody's fool – and no kind of fool at all! Twelve
years of age and already a skilled inventor. His Gyro Gearloose
career began last winter with the observation that every time
his sister got in the car to go somewhere, she had to sit on a freez-
ing child seat. "That's not right!" her big brother thought to
himself and promptly invented a way to redirect the warm air
from the car's heaters to the child seat.

Instead of complaining about a problem, it's smarter to solve
it. This is what Christoph has learned at his grammar school,
the Maristengymnasium, in Fürstenzell, the first school in the
world to put inventing in the school timetable as an optional
subject back in 1982. Electrical engineer Manfred Koser gives two
hours of voluntary teaching a week, showing his pupils the
basics of electrical and mechanical engineering and computer-
assisted tasks. Whereupon he lets them loose with screwdrivers,
saws and welding equipment. "Children's heads are not stuffed
full of conventional wisdom," Koser emphasizes, "so they're
often able to produce surprising ideas." And impressive ones,
too! "I invented a new electric toothbrush head," recounts
12-year-old Jan, "which lets you brush your teeth really well even
if you're wearing a brace." A well-known manufacturer has
already declared an interest in his invention. The fact that many
women have trouble finding what they want in their handbags
inspired 12-year-old Eva: "The inside lining of my bag is made of
Velcro, which lets you fix your keys and your purse in a particular position so you can find them easily again." The child inventors from Fürstenzell regularly carry off national and international prizes – the last few years have brought five gold medals,
six silver and one bronze at the iENA in Nuremberg, the world's
biggest inventions fair.

To free up their minds for new ideas,
the children begin each lesson in teams
by welding little figures. "The best
ideas come to us when we are working
together." Over 250 of the Fürstenzell
pupils' inventions have been awarded
prizes by 'Jugend forscht,' Germany's
Young Scientist of the Year competition.

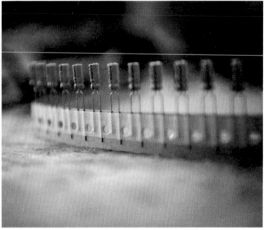

The origin of the conferences was an initiative by Lindau doctors Hein (left) und Parade, together with Count Lennart Bernadotte (centre), member of the Swedish royal family and master of Mainau Island.

The (young) spirit of Lindau

To be allowed to show your work to a real Nobel Prizewinner is the dream of every young scientist. And, every year, it comes true for some of them. In Lindau on Lake Constance. For a week every summer since 1951, a host of Nobel prizewinners assemble with the elite of tomorrow. In master classes, young researchers discuss their ideas with their idols. They profit in two ways – firstly, from the experience of prizewinning researchers and, secondly, from the ideas of their contemporary colleagues. "One of the key successes of Lindau is bridging cultures and distance and initiating thousands of relationships amongst the world's brightest young scientists," observes Brian P. Schmidt (b. 1967), the 2011 Nobel Prizewinner for Physics. So how about going for a coffee with a Nobel Prizewinner or two – or three! The only place to do this is in this Bavarian town on Lake Constance. "People all over the world talk about Lindau and how they would like to emulate it," is how Richard R. Ernst (b. 1933), 1991 Nobel Prizewinner for chemistry, describes the oft-quoted spirit of Lindau. "But few of them ever match up to Lindau."

Bavaria and its Nobel Prizewinners

Over thirty researchers and writers who won one of the coveted prizes sponsored by Alfred Nobel (1833–1896) were born in the Free State, studied here or spent a decisive part of their scientific careers in Bavaria.

Wilhelm Conrad Röntgen (1845–1923)
Physics 1901
Würzburg University
LMU Munich

Hermann Emil Fischer (1852–1919)
Chemistry 1902
Würzburg and Erlangen Universities

Adolf von Baeyer (1835–1917)
Chemistry 1905
LMU Munich

Eduard Buchner (1860–1917)
Chemistry 1907
Würzburg University

Paul Heyse (1830–1914)
Literature 1910

Wilhelm Wien (1864–1928)
Physics 1911
Würzburg University,
LMU Munich

Max von Laue (1879–1960)
Physics 1914
LMU Munich

Richard Willstätter (1872–1942)
Chemistry 1915
LMU Munich

Johannes Stark (1874 –1957)
Physics 1919
Würzburg University

Heinrich Wieland (1877–1957)
Chemistry 1927
LMU Munich,
TU Munich

Ludwig Quidde (1858–1941)
Nobel Peace Prize 1927
Bavarian Academy of Sciences

Thomas Mann (1875–1955)
Literature 1929

Hans Fischer (1881–1945)
Chemistry 1930
TU Munich

Werner Heisenberg (1901–1976)
Physics 1932
LMU Munich,
Bavarian Academy of Sciences

Hans Spemann (1869–1941)
Medicine/
Physiology 1935
LMU Munich,
Würzburg University

Adolf Butenandt (1903–1995)
Chemistry 1939
LMU Munich, President of the Max Planck Society Munich

Rudolf Mößbauer (1929–2011)
Physics 1961
TU Munich

Feodor Lynen (1911–1979)
Medicine/
Physiology 1964
LMU Munich

Ernst Otto Fischer (1918–2007)
Chemistry 1973
TU Munich

Karl von Frisch (1886–1982)
Medicine/
Physiology 1973
LMU Munich

Konrad Lorenz (1903–1989)
Medicine/
Physiology 1973
Max Planck Institute for Behavioural Psychology

Henry Kissinger (b. 1923)
Nobel Peace Prize 1973

Arno Allen Penzias (b. 1933)
Physics 1978

Georges Köhler (1946–1995)
Medicine/
Physiology 1984

Klaus von Klitzing (b. 1943)
Physics 1985
Würzburg University,
TU Munich

Jack Steinberger (b. 1921)
Physics 1988

Johann Deisenhofer (b. 1943)
Chemistry 1988
TU Munich

Robert Huber (b. 1937)
Chemistry 1988
Max Planck Institute for Biochemistry in Martinsried

Hartmut Michel (b. 1948)
Chemistry 1988
Würzburg University

Erwin Neher (b. 1944)
Medicine/
Physiology 1991
TU Munich

Theodor W. Hänsch (b. 1941)
Physics 2005
LMU Munich

Gerhard Ertl (b. 1936)
Chemistry 2007
TU Munich

Konstantin Grcic, born in Munich in 1965. In 2006, Munich's *Haus der Kunst* (House of Art) mounted an exhibition of works by the internationally-acclaimed industrial designer. Grcic's 'Chair One,' designed for Magis, is as solid as a throne and as airy as a cloud (centre). Minimalist form confronts unusual functionality – 'Authentics 2 Hands,' a modern variant of the wicker basket (bottom left).

on/off
konstantin grcic
industrial design
hausderkunst
16/03/06
09/07/06

How a golden generation of industrial designers
came to emerge in Munich

The home of beautiful things

Munich-born Konstantin Grcic is one of the most important contemporary industrial designers and recipient of the
highest honours in his trade. The Chicago Art Institute's
first exhibition on the theme of design, in 2009, was dedicated exclusively to his work. Some of his pieces are in the permanent collection of the MoMA in New York.

Grcic and others have turned Munich into Germany's
design capital. Nearly everything classified as new German
industrial design is created here. While Grcic is the best-
known Munich designer, the list of his prominent colleagues
is now quite long. Two of his former students, Stefan Diez
and Clemens Weisshaar, also work here, both of them established figures on the world stage of industrial design. And
a third generation is already following in their footsteps on
the Isar River, including Steffen Kehrle, a student of Stefan
Diez', who started up on his own a few years ago. A family tree
of the Munich design scene would show Grcic as the patri-
arch of an ever-increasing number of branches, all firmly
rooted in Munich. But why is this so?

Above Grcic's atelier in Schillerstraße, there is a kind
of library of his best-known works, such as 'Chair One' and
'360,' chairs once seen and never again forgotten. Their inventor sits on one of them and explains that, "it wasn't any
conscious decision to live in Munich. That just happened."
Whereupon he smiles and switches the subject suddenly to
Munich's Olympic Park – a success, still fresh and part of the
present. The 1972 Olympic Games made Munich "something
more than it had been before," says Grcic. Into a modern
city "by virtue of its architecture and urban planning." The
city made it easy for him to live here. "It's a question of how
things work here."

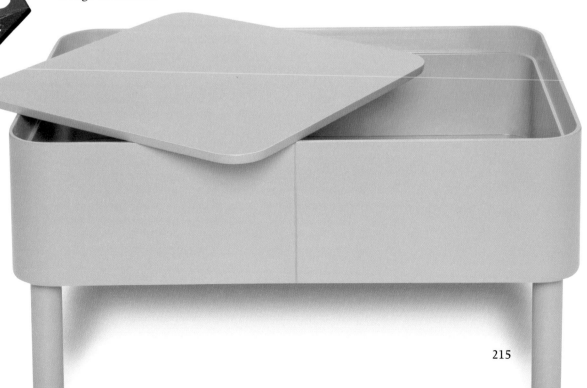

In Munich's Glockenbach
quarter is the atelier of
Swabian-born Steffen Kehrle,
seen here with footballing
friends. His 'Anything' wooden
shelf unit has impressive
side panels with a zigzag profile, allowing shelves to be
inserted at any height (top).
Pretty practical – the Game
coffee table top slides open to
permit storage space (left).

215

Design creates quality of life – a solitaire preparation and presentation element, created by bulthaup design team with Ana Relvão. Ana Relvão, born in Portugal, has a workshop in Munich.

A good fifteen minutes' walk from Grcic's atelier brings us to the Munich Pinakothek der Moderne, the gallery whose New Collection is viewed around the world as the most important assembly of industrial design creations. What they all have in common is their functionality. Florian Hufnagl was the collection's director for 34 years and it is his life's work. "Design," he says, "is a question of tackling a problem. Design is the link between a person and a product. A design is only good if it can also be used." It is thus not merely incidental for industrial designers to prefer an environment that also functions well. It would appear that Munich is a well-designed city which – as Grcic says – makes it easy for him to live here.

Another reason that Munich is home to so many successful industrial designers is its airport. Without being rude to the city itself, the life of a modern industrial designer can often require them to be in three different cities in the space of five days, which means a good local airport is essential. Stefan Diez can confirm this – ten years ago, he started his own business and emancipated himself from the work of his mentor, Grcic. His designs for Thonet, for example, declare his love for the material wood; Diez trained to be a carpenter and his parents ran a joinery business.

The manufacturers for whom Diez works are drawn closer to the city by virtue of its airport – the model builders, metalworkers and deep drawers have already arrived, setting up their premises in the Munich area and supplying the drafts and prototypes which link the chain from idea to product. In a way, the industrial designers share these businesses with one another. These crafts represent a cultural heritage developed over time, born of accumulated expertise and passed

The chair king – Stefan Diez in the Munich atelier which he shares with his wife, jewellery designer Saskia Diez. The Rope Trick lamp designed by Stefan Diez for Wrong for Hay can be converted using a 'rope trick' from a reading light into a ceiling light (left).

down through generations. This appreciation of genuine quality is a genetic characteristic of Munich. The Nymphenburg Porcelain Manufactory is just such an example. A tradition spanning centuries does not dampen the ambition to keep up with the times. The manufactory collaborates with artists and designers on a regular basis, always aiming to improve its own knowledge and ability – something which Diez identifies as a further hallmark of quality.

Ana Relvão gave up her office in Lisbon to study under Diez. Then, the Portuguese designer decided to stay on. Vital and exciting is how she describes Munich's intimate relationship with its industry and the enormous technical competence displayed by colleagues and businesses here. And she still recalls the summer day she fell in love with the city – the whole team was down by the Isar River. They had been swimming and were about to have a picnic. "Where else can you do something like that?"

Munich is certainly not just functional. Munich is also just beautiful. "Functionality alone," explains Florian Hufnagl, "is not enough. There have to be emotions in the mixture, too." Grcic's French colleague, Charlotte Talbot, says, "We designers are, after all, working to improve the quality of life. We're trying to create objects that make life more agreeable. So, designers like us like to work in agreeable surroundings. From this point of view, that makes Munich pretty much the ideal city."

Abridged version of the German article 'Design aus München. Wo die schönen Dinge wohnen' by Alard von Kittlitz, published in ZEITmagazin no. 09/2014, Hamburg, 20 February 2014.

Lamberts Glassworks is the world leader
in mouth-blown plate glass.

"We produce the most modern UV glass in the world."

"When everybody says something can't be done, along comes someone who doesn't know that, and does it." There could hardly be a better description of Reinhard Meindl than this postcard maxim. In 2009, the businessman took the helm of the Waldsassen-based Lamberts Glassworks, one of the world's last remaining manufactories versed in the noble art of glassblowing. "I was the only one there who didn't know how it was done," recalls the 57-year-old with a cheeky grin. But his fresh pair of eyes were just what the craft needed to find a way forward. At his first specialist trade fair, the man from Upper Palatinate observed how "many of the windows were covered with yellow film," which was needed, he was informed, to protect works of art on display in museums and churches and other buildings from ultraviolet rays. The resourceful businessman promptly asked himself, "Why don't they just incorporate the ultraviolet protection straight into the glass?" The experts rejected his idea. "It won't work, believe us." But Meindl refused to let his idea go without a fight. He and his staff set about experimenting, and countless failed attempts followed. "But the team hung on," Meindl recounts with pride. Every test brought a re-think, followed by another test, until it finally worked out. "After two years, we had developed a mouth-blown type of glass which absorbed ultraviolet rays directly." The world's only UV protective glass has been launched onto the market and its patent is pending. Orders have already been reaching the Upper Palatinate-based glassworks from all parts of the world. When Meindl presented this glass innovation at a fair, the watching experts were stunned. "Oh! It can be done, then!"

Lamberts Glassworks have been producing mouth-blown glass since 1934. Their manufacturing processes and tools have a tradition going back 350 years. Whether for glass objects or church windows, there are over 5000 colours and a wide range of textures for their customers to choose from. The manufactory's self-supporting wooden construction, built in 1896, is also unique and is a listed building.

At the multi-generation house in Haßfurt, everybody helps everybody else – mothers bring their babies to the crèche, volunteers advise senior citizens on how to use laptops and mobile phones; in Helga Koeppe's eurythmy course, Alysha balances on a beam (bottom). Regardless of the background, music and crafts groups bring indigenous and immigrant families closer together (right-hand page).

Lower Franconian symbiosis – the Haßfurt
multi-generation house

"Every person has a particular talent."

Her braided pigtail whips through the air like a lasso. Her floral ballet pumps slap and shuffle across the floor. With flute music playing in the background, 8-year-old Alysha leaps like Bambi through the first snows of winter across the dance studio floor at the multi-generation house in Haßfurt. "She used to be very reserved," recounts her grandma, Ulrike Brandl. Things have been different since Alysha began attending Helga Koeppe's eurythmy class. In her flowing fairy dress, the 78-year-old holds therapeutic movement art sessions with children, adults and senior citizens. She teaches from the heart, for the soul – for her participants' souls and for her own.

This is one of many symbioses in the multi-generation house on Haßfurt's market square. Run by the Red Cross since 2008, the facility is a meeting-place for people from every background or age group, where a modern approach can be breathed into the principle of the extended family and young and old can learn from one another throughout its four floors. There's dancing in the basement and a German course in the loft. When it's busy, there's something happening on every floor; the permutations are endless.

The three full-time ladies on the staff organize activities – usually for free – from nine in the morning till nine in the evening, whether it's a crèche for toddlers or a computer course for pensioners, recreation for kids or advice on dementia. It's mainly volunteers who offer their services – often for their own enjoyment, too. "Anyone can contribute their time and talent and at the same time learn from others," is coordinator Gudrun Greger's comment on the house's concept. This Lower Franconian pilot project demonstrates that no-one has to fear growing old or being alone as long as we integrate more such facilities into the heart of our communities. There is no better proof of that than the smiling faces of Helga Koeppe and Alysha.

Well, look at that!

Almost 20 000 people in Bavaria work in **optical technologies,** one of Germany's twelve key technology fields. The field includes laser technology, optical manufacturing, optical metrology and optical sensor technology as well as optical ICT. Players located in the Free State include Ficosa and its subsidiary Adasens Automotive, Agfa-Gevaert HealthCare, Sill Optik, Osram Opto Semiconductors, Menlo Systems and Toptica Photonics.

Where is the home of the **digital future?** In **Munich.** The EU's 2014 *ICT Hotspot Atlas* puts the city on the Isar in first place, ahead of London and Paris. The information and communications technology rankings encompassed 133 regions across Europe. Bavaria is investing a total of 1.8 billion euros in advancing the progress of the digital era – more than any other state in Germany.

Alois Alzheimer (1864–1915), the doctor, psychiatrist and neuropathologist from Marktbreit in Lower Franconia, ranks among the most important figures in the history of medicine. In 1906, when treating Auguste Deter, he was the first to describe the illness dementia, signalling the dawn of research into the still-incurable Alzheimer's disease.

In 2012, energy-related CO_2 **emissions** in the Free State stood at six tons per capita, and thus a third lower than the national average of nine tons. By way of comparison, the figure for the USA was 17 tons.

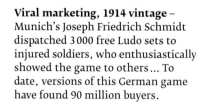

Viral marketing, 1914 vintage – Munich's Joseph Friedrich Schmidt dispatched 3 000 free Ludo sets to injured soldiers, who enthusiastically showed the game to others... To date, versions of this German game have found 90 million buyers.

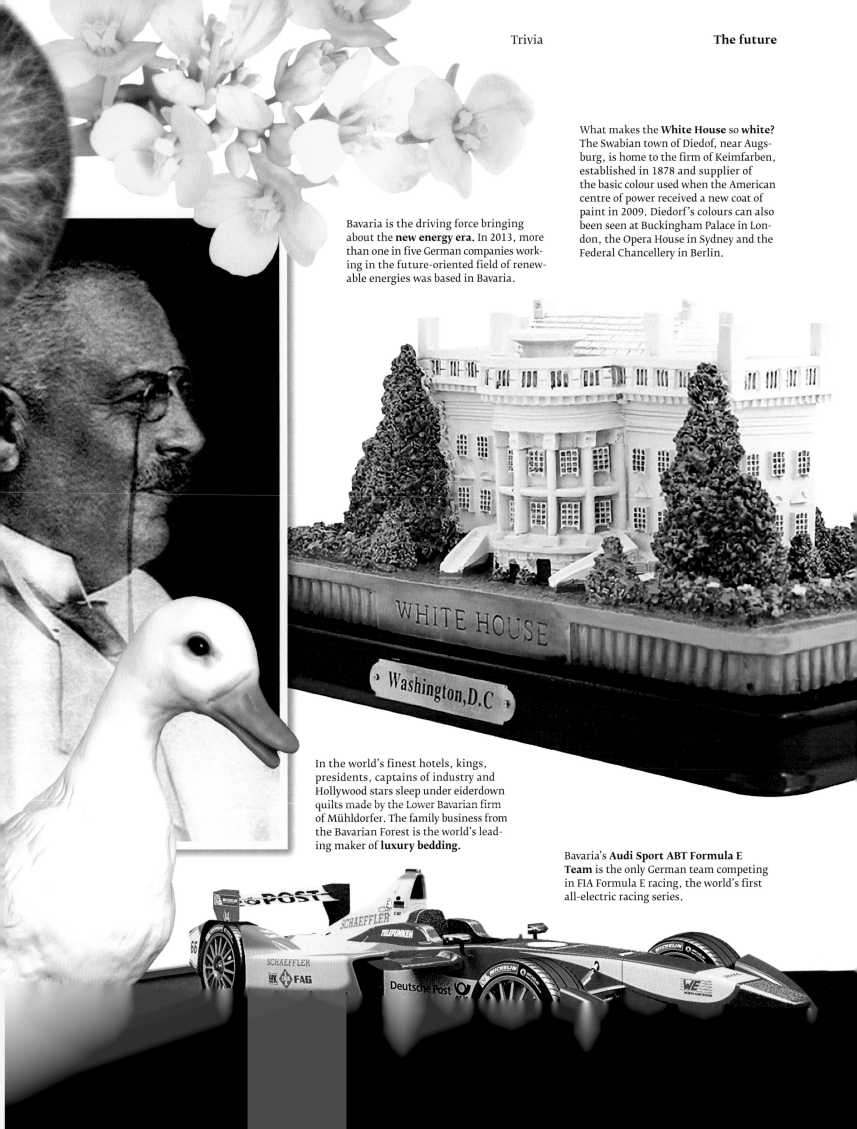

What makes the **White House** so **white?** The Swabian town of Diedof, near Augsburg, is home to the firm of Keimfarben, established in 1878 and supplier of the basic colour used when the American centre of power received a new coat of paint in 2009. Diedorf's colours can also been seen at Buckingham Palace in London, the Opera House in Sydney and the Federal Chancellery in Berlin.

Bavaria is the driving force bringing about the **new energy era.** In 2013, more than one in five German companies working in the future-oriented field of renewable energies was based in Bavaria.

In the world's finest hotels, kings, presidents, captains of industry and Hollywood stars sleep under eiderdown quilts made by the Lower Bavarian firm of Mühldorfer. The family business from the Bavarian Forest is the world's leading maker of **luxury bedding.**

Bavaria's **Audi Sport ABT Formula E Team** is the only German team competing in FIA Formula E racing, the world's first all-electric racing series.

Bavaria and the world in the year 2050

The world stands at a crossroads in its history. Our planet's climate is under threat, raw materials are running low, energy supplies must be reorganized on a new, sustainable basis. Electricity, very efficiently produced, transported and used, becomes the universal energy source. In addition, a new age of automation and digitalization dawns – a thousand-fold increase in computing power, storage capacity and microchip data transfer rates is to be expected over the next 30 years. By the year 2050, the number of people living in cities will be as great as today's total world population, and, for the first time, there will be more elderly people than children and adolescents. This is why we have never before been so reliant on researchers and engineers, doctors, urban planners and politicians to find creative solutions – smart power grids and buildings will be needed, as will computers to assist doctors, energy-trading buildings, natural light from ceilings, power plants in the basement or on the roof or out at sea; so will pea-sized mainframe computers, virtual universities and three-dimensional internet worlds. None of this is merely a vision; it is a reality almost within reach. Munich's Siemens AG is working on all these innovative projects. The staff at the technology company's seventeen locations in Bavaria are already working to create the future – for Bavaria and for the world.

An African city in the year 2060, with real-time collation of damaged road surfaces, railway lines or power stations followed by prompt repairs.

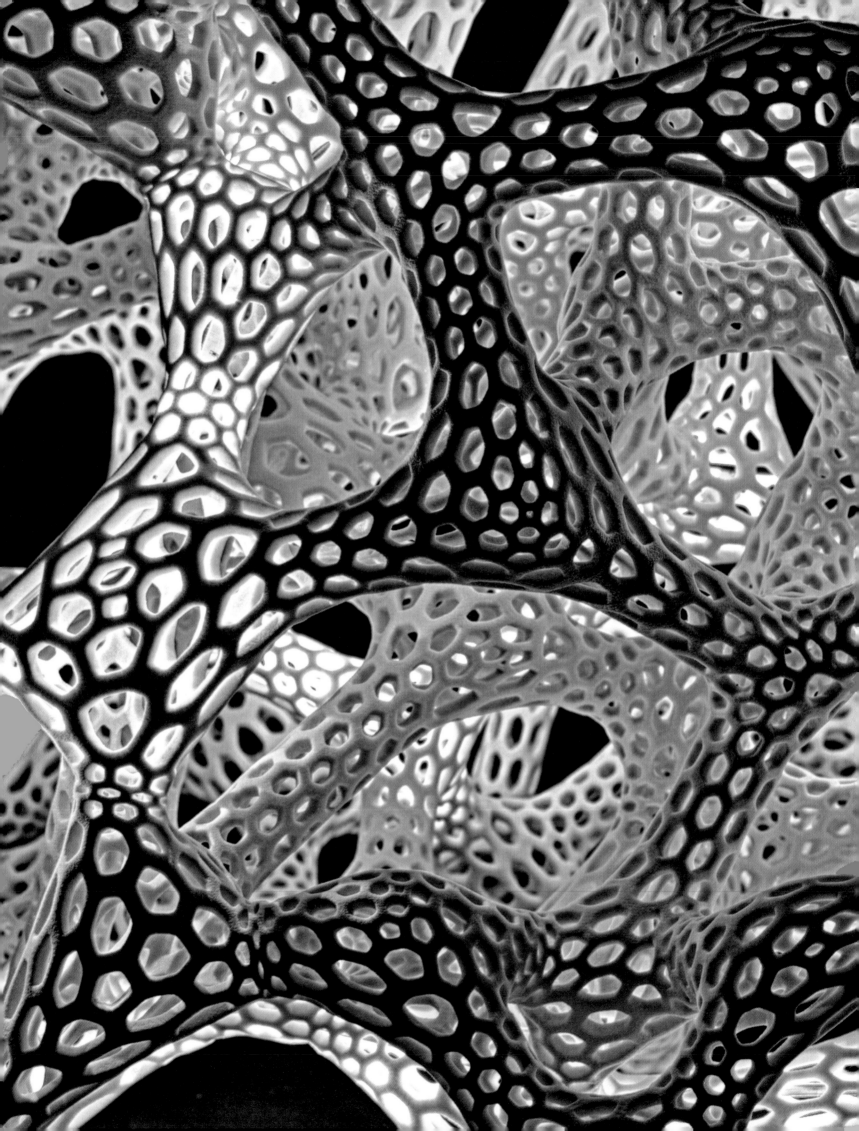

A new world at the push of a button

The first house in the world to be produced using a 3-D printer, complete with toilet area, kitchen worktop and furniture. voxeljet, a firm based in Friedberg, near Augsburg, took a mere 60 hours to 'print off' architect Peter Ebner's design. Set up by Munich's Technical University, the Swabia-based company claims to possess the world's largest 3-D printer. For the James Bond film, *Skyfall,* voxeljet supplied three Aston Martins to double the vintage cars of the sixties. It wasn't the irreplaceable originals but three cheap print-up models that went up in flames. And the car industry is also beginning to take more advantage of economical 3-D prototypes. Car parts, furniture and architectural models straight from the printer – what sounds like science fiction is just the push of a button away. 3-D printing technology may be set to revolutionize the production processes of entire industries, as expensive tools can be done away with. As one of the world's leading 3-D printing specialists, voxeljet intends to have a hand in shaping that revolution – from its base in Bavaria.

As good as the original, and visually hard to tell apart – off-the-printer, James Bond actor Daniel Craig's Aston Martin.

Turning knowledge to good use

Knowledge is power. Supercomputers and high-performance software are capable of filtering, organizing and interlinking enormous quantities of data – far faster and more comprehensively than humans ever could – and this will make basic research easier. Split-second data analyses also help to optimize production processes and supply chains – weak links can be identified and removed in real time. Musical trends can also be recognized more quickly, which should please fans. And when it comes to directing traffic more easily or predicting the weather or some megatrend-in-the-making, the world's fastest analytical in-memory database system has to be a big help. And that help comes from Nuremberg-based EXASOL AG.

Picking up trends in music even faster,
and getting them on the stage – for example,
at Rock in the Park in Nuremberg.

Mobility in the future

With its powerful research base and mighty carmaking industry, Bavaria has the means to continue producing the world's best cars. Carmakers will shortly be testing innovative assistance systems on a high-tech motorway connecting Munich and Nuremberg.

To this end, Audi is improving road safety with highly-automated, piloted driving. In the event of any danger, cars will forewarn each other. Audi is developing resource-saving technologies like 'Ampelinfo online' to help cars move at just the right speed to encounter one green light after another and thus save on fuel (see picture). Urban planners and carmakers intend to link data from infrastructural elements with vehicles.

BMW plans to support the driver of the future using systems which facilitate driving or, if desired, even take over the task of driving completely. A car will become a communications hub providing high-speed data access enabling the driver to surf, mail and confer. Car-sharing in major urban centres – using emission-free vehicles – will be a theme of growing importance for the BMW Group, where priority is now being given to multimodal concepts which will link multiple means of transport.

The car of the future will run on regeneratively-produced electricity, and it will be quiet, cheap, exhaust-free and non-dependent on oil. One of the challenges involved is to produce an affordable electric car for everyday use. A major step in this direction has been made by Munich Technical University researchers in collaboration with industry experts. They have developed the Visio M, an efficient, nippy little electric two-seater car which is much lighter and smaller than other e-cars and only half as costly to buy and run. Not counting its battery, the car weighs in at just 450 kilogrammes, can reach a speed of around 75 mph and has a range of about 100 miles. The Visio M is still only a prototype made of carbon-fibre-reinforced plastic. Serial production will require the researchers to adapt its components to mass-production conditions. If they are successful, the Visio M could come onto the market in 2020.

An urban runaround –
Munich's Technical University has developed
the Visio M compact electric car.

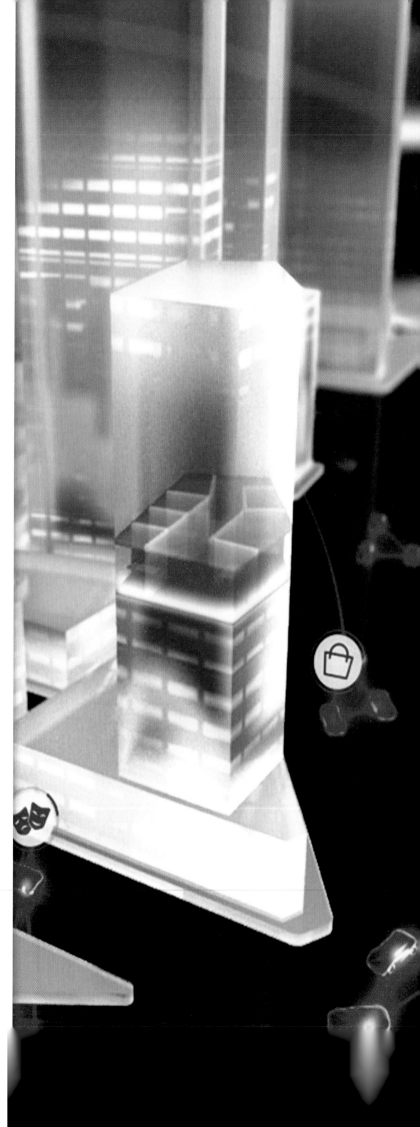

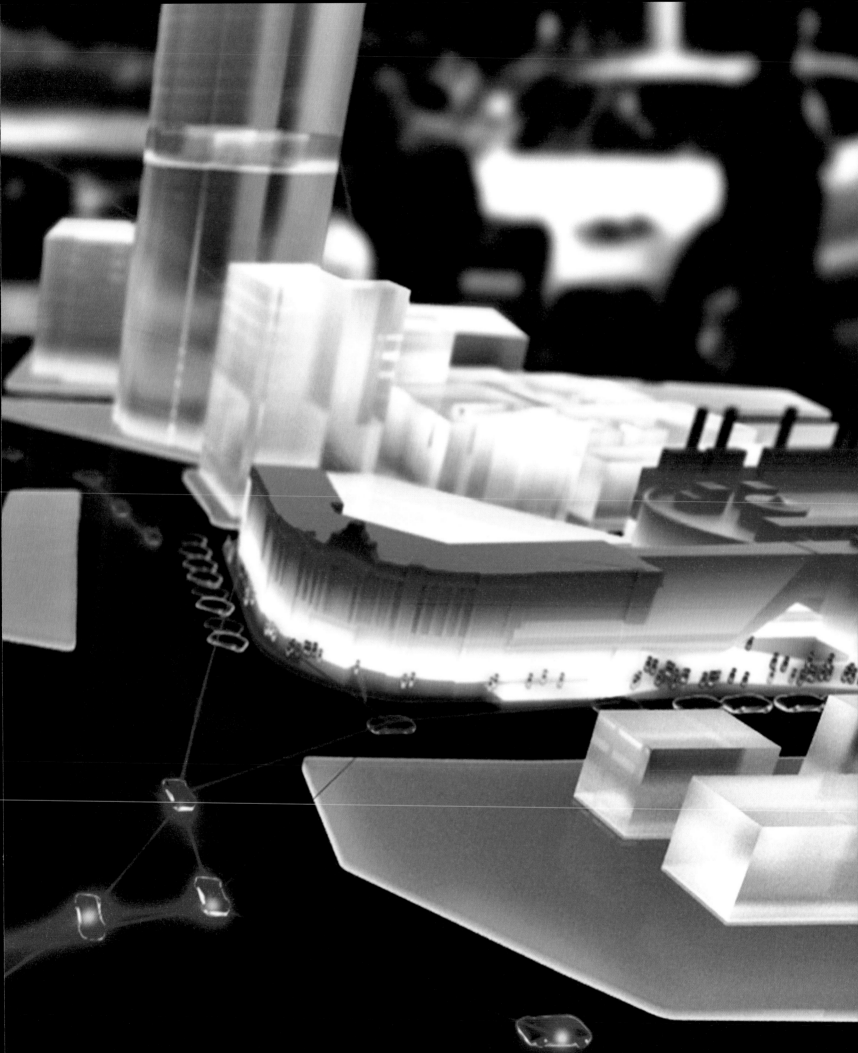

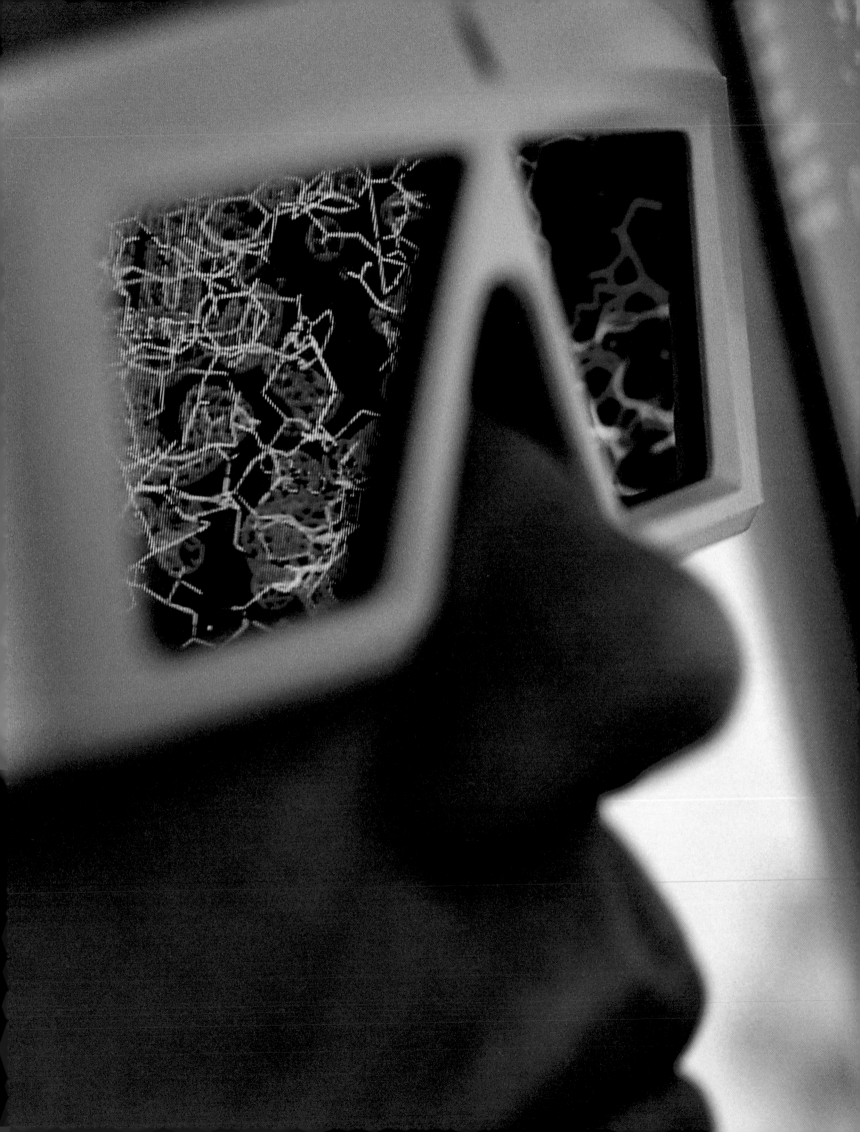

Making data networks secure

The 21st century's version of gold is virtual data, and, in the same way that gold has always had to be guarded closely, information on companies and private individuals has to be safeguarded as it travels and parks along the digital highways. To prevent cyber theft and other cyber crimes, the data networks used by professionals and home users must be made as burglar-proof as possible. German and, in particular, Bavarian companies working in this field enjoy a worldwide competence in data protection. The Kirchheim-based firm genua mbH near Munich is researching into the creation of a digital signature which cannot be deciphered even by the high-capacity quantum computers that will be available in the future.

Web-based remote servicing of (ships') engines or IT systems only saves time and expense if networks are reliably protected from external attacks.

Storing renewable energy

Whenever the sun is shining or the wind is blowing, an enormous quantity of renewable energy is being produced, regardless of how much is actually being consumed. And as long as the wind is going to blow when it pleases and the sun refuses to be turned on and off according to demand, renewable energy will need to be stored safely and over long periods. A large number of researchers and companies in Bavaria are searching for solutions. Among them is Hydrogenious Technologies GmbH, based in Erlangen, a spin-off from the FAU Friedrich-Alexander-Universität Erlangen-Nürnberg. Their idea is to store surplus solar and wind power as hydrogen suspended in an easy-to-use carrier solution. The advantage of using such economical suspensions is that they can be transported in conventional tanks and enable homes and other buildings to avail themselves of their own reliable supply of energy.

The 2014 Renewable Energies Study comparing Germany's states confirmed Bavaria's undisputed position as leader in the field of photovoltaics.

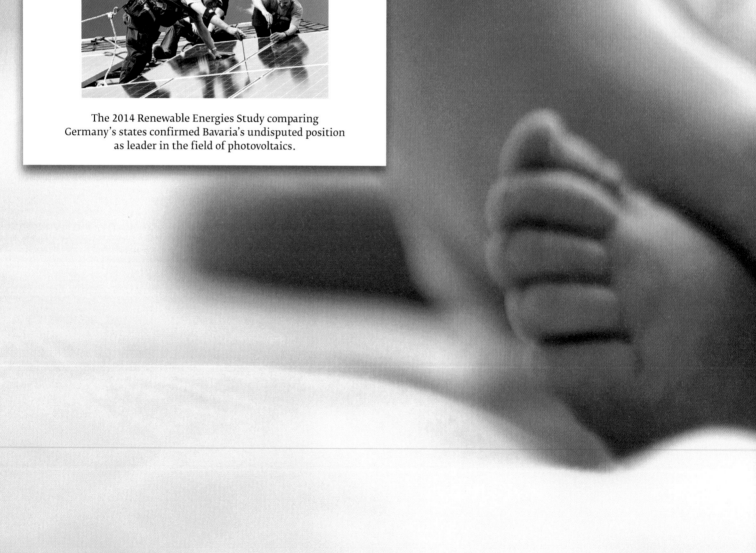

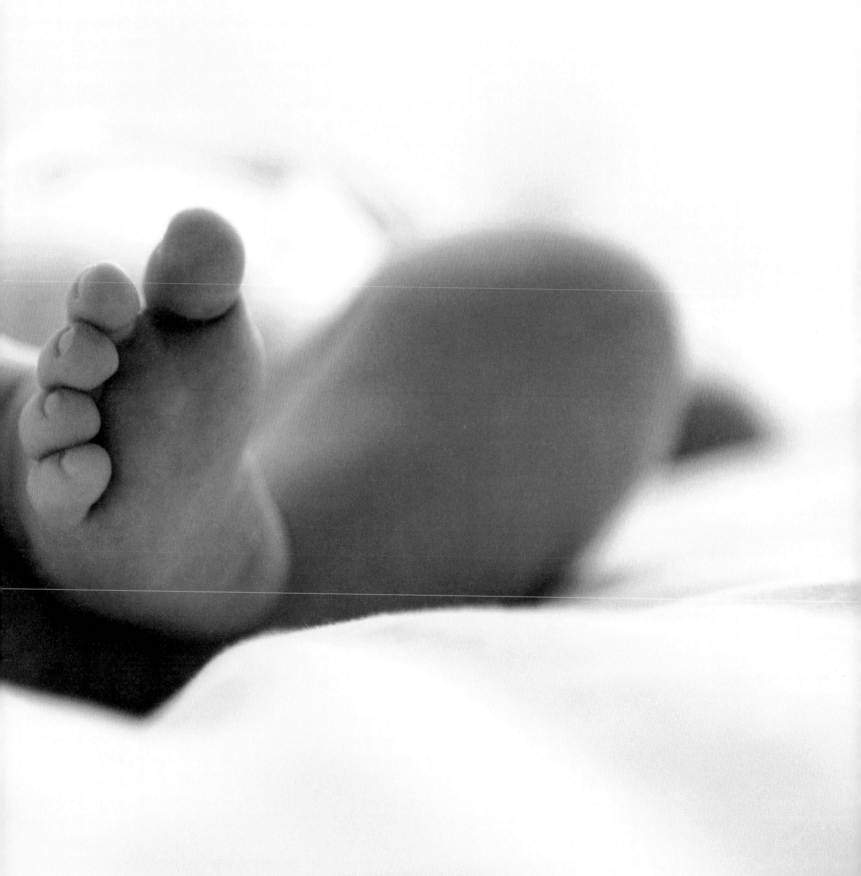

Things think, too

The fourth revolution is well underway. First, production was mechanized, then electrified and more recently automated. We have now entered the age of Industrial Internet of Things, where the physical world is set to merge with the virtual. Smart factories are producing smart products, things that can think. Every machine and production module is networked and can communicate with every other. A customer orders a product, and the factory begins production, whereby each production part carries microchips with instructions telling the machine what to do with it. Intelligent assembly-line robots read the instructions, carry them out and report any defects. In this way, the production process runs itself, flexibly and under human supervision. The embedded computers have to be programmed and networked with all the electronic and mechanical production components. The necessary know-how equates to a clear-cut innovative head start in the new industrial age, and it's the kind of know-how available at Heitec AG, a company from the Middle Franconian city of Erlangen which provides a specialized range of software, mechanical and electronics services and has already developed and successfully implemented more than 250 Industrial Internet of Things-related projects around the world.

The factory of the future can only be as smart as its robots. Sensitive and complex assembly tasks present no obstacles to the world's first touch-sensitive lightweight robot, skillfully produced by Augsburg-based company KUKA AG, one of the world's leading robot and plant constructors and a major driving force in the development of robot workforces. Their robots can work in direct contact with humans with no need for any protective barriers, relieving staff of dangerous or physically strenuous tasks.

KUKA's lightweight robot is so sensitive that it recoils automatically when touched.

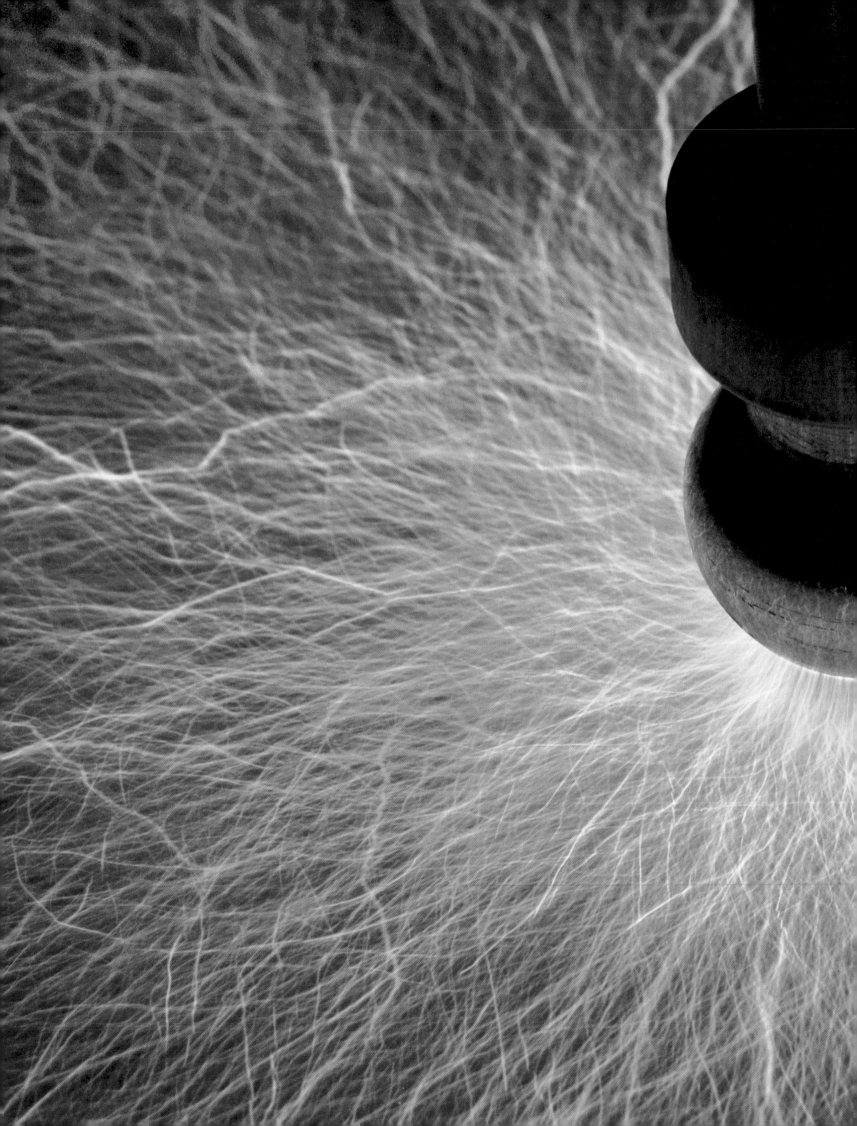

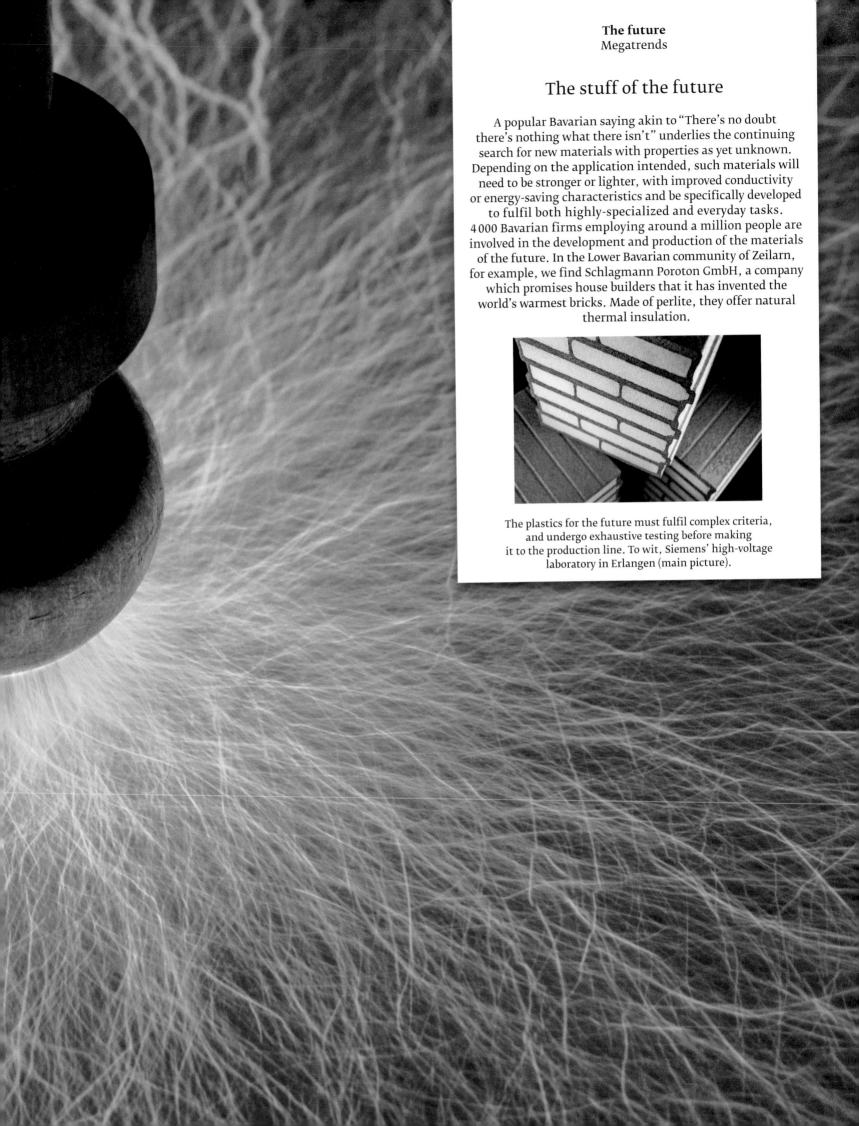

The stuff of the future

A popular Bavarian saying akin to "There's no doubt there's nothing what there isn't" underlies the continuing search for new materials with properties as yet unknown. Depending on the application intended, such materials will need to be stronger or lighter, with improved conductivity or energy-saving characteristics and be specifically developed to fulfil both highly-specialized and everyday tasks. 4 000 Bavarian firms employing around a million people are involved in the development and production of the materials of the future. In the Lower Bavarian community of Zeilarn, for example, we find Schlagmann Poroton GmbH, a company which promises house builders that it has invented the world's warmest bricks. Made of perlite, they offer natural thermal insulation.

The plastics for the future must fulfil complex criteria, and undergo exhaustive testing before making it to the production line. To wit, Siemens' high-voltage laboratory in Erlangen (main picture).

The future of building

More than a billion of the world's people have no access to clean drinking water, while 2.6 billion are not connected up to any water supply and waste disposal system. New water recycling technologies may help not only to solve these problems but also to ensure that water is managed more sustainably. The future will witness more and more people living in urban areas, needing fresh air, clean water – and a reliable energy supply as well. In the environmentally-responsible and resource-efficient buildings of the future known as Green Buildings, energy and water will be managed highly efficiently. There are Bavarian companies already producing such solutions. HUBER SE, for example, is a company located in Berching in Upper Palatinate who provide a means of recovering the heat energy present in waste water, which would otherwise be flushed away after showering, bathing, washing or rinsing. The energy thus recovered can be used to heat the building according to climate-friendly principles. In 2010, the Lower Bavarian city of Straubing kicked off Germany's first pilot project, using Huber technology, aimed at delivering 'heating drawn from the sewers.' Waste water from the municipal sewage plant now provides 102 homes with 65 per cent of their heating.

Protecting nature sustainably – Energy-efficient and fully accessible, Berchtesgaden's House of the Mountains (large photo) is a unique environmental experience.

Bavaria and the world
in the year 2030

Forecasts and expectations formulated in the past have shown us that our perception of the future is always limited by the means of assessment available to us in the present. One thing, however, is certain, and that is that Europe's regions will become more important. In this respect, Bavaria is likely to play a special role by virtue of its establishment as a state within the nation-state context of the Federal Republic of Germany and the fact that, before the present era, it was able to find its place as a regionally-integrated solitaire. Bavaria was never at the centre of the 19th-century industrial revolution, but it is doubtless in the vanguard of new technological developments and their implementation in economic and business models.

Bavaria is not only a European region at the heart of the coming industrial revolution; it has also undergone a process of social modernization. The Free State has become both more 'German' and more international. It is characterized by its status as a net recipient of both internal immigrants and individuals and families from elsewhere in Europe and beyond. None of these modern developments have come at the cost of Bavaria's traditional self-confidence, a feature which, to outside observers, contributes greatly to its attractiveness.

Its belated and thus more modern development is indisputably a locational advantage, and Bavaria is certain to have profited by 2030 from having been able – unlike more traditional industrial heartlands – to start many things anew and at the same time draw on its traditional self-assurance. The Free State is destined to assume a pivotal role, given that it is blessed with the best prerequisites for such modernization – it is certainly economically buoyant, but other factors are also at play: its population has become more diverse, even beyond its major urban centres; it is a hub of educational quality and scholarship; and it can of course look proudly on a grandiose cultural history, going back to Ludwig I, which has developed in leaps and bounds in recent decades.

Social coexistence will increasingly be characterized by the extent to which new ways of working, a more plural society and more exacting demands placed on general and vocational education are able to accommodate one another. We already know that the new technological and business megatrends will deliver more than just quantitative growth; we can also expect qualitative changes to reach into even our most private spheres of activity. We should understand that modernizing the way we live is not simply an improvement as such; the more diverse society of the future will require us to sound out a new appreciation of regional identities. The intricately more complex and globalized future will require us not to neglect the need to evolve predictable social constructs.

These are the challenges to be met not only by Bavaria, but it may be that Bavaria will, in view of the ideal economic, cultural, educational and social circumstances it enjoys, be expected to act as a special role model within Europe for sustainable modernization processes. The principal social challenges facing every part of Europe will consist not simply in holding their own on world markets but also in creating viable societal structures capable of coping adequately with the socially-disadvantaged in their own regions. Bavaria's position of relative strength may enable it not to lose sight of its disadvantaged citizens.

We should picture the Bavaria of 2030 as we do today as a place whose self-awareness and cultural roots draw on a tradition far more authentic than the mere folkloristic. This self-awareness should be deployed to promote a cosmopolitan ethos which is suited to the needs of people of different ethnic and social backgrounds, and which evolves out of economic, scientific and cultural creativity. Few other places are as well-endowed as Bavaria for this purpose. Perhaps cosmopolitanism and self-awareness can only exist in a complementary relationship! The Bavaria of 2030 will certainly be a Bavarian one – but also more German, more European and more global than it is today. That need not be a contradiction in terms, as the Bavaria of today already demonstrates.

Armin Nassehi (b. 1960), Professor of Sociology,
Ludwig-Maximilians-Universität Munich

The Bavarian Anthem

Gott mit dir, du Land der Bayern, deutsche Erde, Vaterland!
Über deinen weiten Gauen ruhe Seine Segenshand!
Er behüte deine Fluren, schirme deiner Städte Bau
Und erhalte dir die Farben Seines Himmels, weiß und blau!

Gott mit dir, dem Bayernvolke, dass wir, uns'rer Väter wert,
fest in Eintracht und in Frieden bauen uns'res Glückes Herd!
Dass mit Deutschlands Bruderstämmen einig uns ein jeder schau
und den alten Ruhm bewähre unser Banner, weiß und blau!

God be with you, Bavarian state, German soil and fatherland!
Your broad regions blessed by His gentle hand.
Your rolling fields may He guard, your tall cities, too,
And keep the colours of His heaven, our white and blue!

God be with you, Bavarian nation. Our fathers may we please,
Our fortune forge midst harmony and peace.
May all see us, to our German brothers true,
And, proclaiming ancient glories, our banner white and blue!

Illustration credits

Opening pages and other motifs:
pp. 2/3, 12/13, 16/17, 24/25, 102, 158/159: Kilian Schönberger

p. 4: Thomas Plettenberg

pp. 6–11, 39 (bottom): Steffen Egly

pp. 14–15, 18–21, 53: Die Neue Sammlung – The International Design Museum Munich: Entrance to the permanent exhibition Design at the Pinakothek der Moderne (bottom), 186/187: Manuel Irritier

Testimonials/Portraits:
pp. 66/67, 86–87, 94/95, 100/101, 104/105, 108, 112/113, 116/117, 119, 122 (top), 124/125, 130/131, 133, 142/143, 150/151, 172/173, 190/191, 199 (top left and bottom), 202/203, 208/209, 210/211, 218–221: Kilian Blees

Graphics/Diagrams
pp. 22/23, 60/61, 76/77, 134/135, 146/147, 242/243: Tina Berning

p. 26: Günter Lenz/Image Broker/Ullsteinbild

p. 27: Marius Walla

p. 28/29: AKG-Images (6)

p. 30: Benediktinerstift Kremsmünster, Josef Leithner

p. 31: Bayerischer Landtag

p. 32: steel engraving: Alexander Marx, 1845; photograph: Hans Grüner

p. 33: wörner traxler richter, planungsgesellschaft mbh, Frankfurt am Main/foyer (top), Haus der Bayerischen Geschichte, Augsburg (bottom)

pp. 34/35: Julius Kramer/Fokusnatur (top left), Berthold Steinhilber/Laif (3)

pp. 36/37: Berthold Steinhilber/Laif

p. 38: Peter von Felbert (top), Look-Foto (bottom)

p. 39: Christoph Gießing (top)

p. 40/41: Heinz Zak

p. 42: Peter von Felbert (top), Marco Heilmann (bottom)

p. 43: Audi museum mobile (top), Gabi Röhrl (bottom)

p. 44: Stefan Schütz/Look-Foto

p. 45: Georg Knoll/Laif (top left), Bayerische Schlösserverwaltung (top right), Florian Werner/Look-Foto (bottom)

pp. 46/47: Wolfram Lindmahr

p. 50: Thomas Ruff, *Substrat 21*, 2002. © VG Bild-Kunst, Bonn 2015 (left); Georg Baselitz, *Fingermalerei III – Adler*, 1972, oil on canvas, (framed) 166 x 134 cm, MKM Museum Küppersmühle für Moderne Kunst, Duisburg, Sammlung Ströher (right)

p. 51: Marcel Odenbach, *In stillen Teichen lauern Krokodile*, 2002/04 Installation Aschemünder/Sammlung Goetz at Haus der Kunst, Courtesy Sammlung Goetz, Medienkunst, München, photography: Wilfried Petzi, Marcel Odenbach, VG Bild-Kunst, Bonn 2015 (top); Hans Madej/Laif (bottom)

p. 52: AKG-Images

p. 53: Image Broker/Mauritius Images (top)

p. 54: travelstock44/Look-Foto (top); Westend 61/Mauritius Images (bottom left); The State Hermitage Museum, St. Petersburg, photography: Konstantin Sinyavskiy (bottom right)

p. 55: ZOOEY BRAUN/Artur Images

p. 56: Haus der Bayerischen Geschichte, Augsburg (top left); Kerster & Co./SZ Photo (top right); Bernd Römmelt/Mauritius Images (middle left); DEA PICTURE LIBRARY/Getty Images (bottom left)

p. 57: Berthold Steinhilber/Laif (top); Erich Lessing/AKG Images (bottom)

pp. 58/59: Michael Boyny/Look-Foto

p. 62: Eugen Peters (top), Dieter Deventer/SZ Photo/Laif (bottom)

pp. 63 and 64: Jens Schwarz/Laif

p. 65: urban beach Würzburg, Elmar Hahn (top left); Tobias Gerber/Laif (top right); Martin Graf (bottom left); Clemens Mayer (bottom right)

p. 68: Bayreuther Festspiele/Enrico Nawrath/DPA/Picture-Alliance (top); Ullsteinbild (bottom)

p. 69: Bayreuther Festspiele/Enrico Nawrath/DPA/Picture-Alliance (2)

pp. 70/71: Bayreuther Festspiele/Jörg Schulze/DPA/Picture-Alliance

p. 72: Andreas Mühlbauer, Furth im Wald (top left); OPEN AIR PUCH 2014, layout: Herburg Weiland, photography: Peter Hetzmannseder (top right); Liu Yin (bottom)

p. 73: Stephan Rumpf/SZ Photo/Picture Alliance (top), Chiemsee Summer (middle right); Uwe Niklas (bottom left); KW NEUN Grafikagentur/www.kw-neun.de (bottom right)

p. 74: "Die Förderer" e.V. Landshut (2)

p. 75: Laura Schweiger (oben), "Die Förderer" e.V. Landshut (unten, 3)

p. 78: DPA/Ullsteinbild (top); Foto: Bildarchiv Deutsches Filminstitut, Bavaria Film 1981 (bottom)

p. 79: Constantin Film 2001 (top); Wiedemann & Berg Film 2006 (bottom left); AMPAS (bottom right)

p. 80: 90060/KPA/SZ photography (top left and bottom); produced by Bayerischer Rundfunk, licence by BRmedia Service GmbH (top right); WDR/Balance Film (middle right)

p. 81: produced by Bayerischer Rundfunk, licence by BRmedia Service GmbH (top right); MFA Filmdistribution e.K. (middle left); Constantin Film 2013 (middle right); Christian Hartmann/Roxy Film 2013 (bottom left); 2001 herbX film/Jürgen Olczyk (bottom right)

pp. 82/83: Fotolia

pp. 84/85: Sonja Allgaier

pp. 88–91: Barbara Bonisolli

p. 92: DPA/Picture Alliance (top), Mediafocus (bottom left); Bayerisches Hauptstaatsarchiv (bottom right)

p. 93: AKG-Images

p. 95: Florian Hammerich (bottom)

pp. 96/97: Andrea Warnecke/DPA/Picture-Alliance (gingerbread), AMPAS (Oscar envelope), The Image Bank/Getty Images (Allianz Arena), Disney (Snow White), Stephan Göschler (plate "zur Hölle"), Andreas Strauß/Look-Foto (Watzmann), Photo Researchers/Getty Images (Einstein), www.nepal-himalaya-pavillon.de (Buddha), iStock/Getty Images Plus (rosary)

pp. 98/99: Simon Katzer/Ullsteinbild

p. 103: Andreas Plenk

p. 109: Bayerischer Rundfunk

p. 110: H. Gruber/Trachtenverein Oberstdorf (top right), Armin Weigel/Picture-Alliance (middle left), Peter von Felbert (bottom), Wildlife (bottom right)

p. 111: Fotolia (top left), Lukas Barth/SZ Photo, Karl-Josef Hildenbrand/DPA/Picture-Alliance (bottom)

p. 118: Lennart Preiss/Getty Images (top left); Armin Weigel/DPA/Picture-Alliance (middle left); Johannes Simon/Getty Images (bottom left); Florian Weichselbaumer (bottom right)

pp. 120/121: Daniel Karmann/DPA/Picture Alliance

p. 122: Jonas Kraus (bottom left), Hubert Lankes for Kapelle Josef Menzl (bottom right)

p. 123: Gerald von Floris (top), Michi Reimers/Jazz Archiv/Picture-Alliance (bottom)

p. 124: private (top right), Arthur Da Costa (bottom right)

p. 126/127: DPA/Picture Alliance

p. 128: DDP/Ullsteinbild (top left), Florian Bachmeier/Image Broker/Ullsteinbild (top right), Hans Madej/Laif (middle left), Stadt Lauingen, Danube (bottom left)

p. 129: age fotostock/LOOK-Foto (top), Berthold Steinhilber/Laif (bottom left), Jan Memmel (bottom right)

p. 132: David Rasche Photography

Seite 136: Getty Images (oben), Staatsgalerie Stuttgart/AKG-Images (unten)

p. 137: Stefan Moses, *Oskar Maria Graf, Starnberger Wald 1964*, from the series "Große Alte im Wald" or "Deutschlands Emigranten"/Courtesy Johanna Breede PHOTOKUNST/1964; AKG-Images (top right)

pp. 138/139: Städtische Galerie im Lenbachhaus und Kunstbau, München, VG Bild-Kunst, Bonn 2015 (left); Timpe/Ullsteinbild (right); AKG-Images (bottom right)

p. 140: Bildarchiv Foto Marburg/Wolf-Christian von der Mülbe, detail of the Baroque fresco, Munich

p. 141: Universal History Archive/Getty Images (top left); Hulton Archive/Getty Images (middle); DEA PICTURE LIBRARY/Getty Images (bottom right)

p. 144: Juergen Teller: *Zwei Schäuferle mit Kloß und eine Kinderportion Schnitzel mit Pommes Frites*, 2002 (oben); Kurt Cobain, Berlin 1991 (unten)

p. 145: Juergen Teller, *Kate Moss, No. 12*, Gloucestershire 2010

p. 148: Barth/Laif (left), Fotolia (right)

p. 149: Hans Madej/Laif (top), Peter von Felbert (bottom)

pp. 152/153: Pedro Miranda

p. 154: Frank Bauer/Contour by Getty Images (top right); Fabrice Coffrini/Getty Images (middle left); FRANÇOIS XAVIER MARIT/Getty Images (bottom left)

p. 155: Nadine Rupp (top right and bottom left); Frank Bauer/Contour by Getty Images (bottom right)

pp. 156/157: Zoiglbauer (logo), Peter Tarnoff/Retna Ltd./Corbis (Jimi Hendrix), DPA/Picture Alliance (football), Barbara Bonisolli (dumpling), Club Mate/Brauerei Loscher (bottle), Science Photo Library/AKG Images (Simon Marius), Haus der Bayerischen Geschichte, Augsburg (Schlierseer folk comedy ensemble), Lebkuchenherz München Schifferl (gingerbread), Fotosearch (bee)

p. 161: Ayzit Bostan

pp. 162/163: drawing: Nicolas-Antoine Taunay, copperplate engraving: George Malbeste, Münchner Stadtmuseum

p. 164: Bayerisches Hauptstaatsarchiv, Bayerischer Landtag 10191 (top); Münchner Stadtmuseum, Collection Graphics/Poster/Paintings (unten)

p. 165: Haus der Bayerischen Geschichte, Augsburg (left); AKG-Images/Picture-Alliance (top right); Staatliche Münzsammlung München, photographer: Nicolai Kästner (bottom)

p. 166: Germaine Krull/Ullsteinbild (top); Walter Ditz, print: Fritz Maison/Haus der Bayerischen Geschichte, Augsburg (bottom)

p. 167: Haus der Bayerischen Geschichte, Augsburg (top); Bayerisches Hauptstaatsarchiv (bottom)

p. 168: Hugo Jaeger/Timepix/The LIFE Picture Collection/Getty Images (top); Sammlung Megele/SZ Photo (bottom)

p. 169: Gamma Rapho (top); Haus der Bayerischen Geschichte, Augsburg, photography: Carl Lamb, April 1945, Bayerisches Landesamt für Denkmalpflege (bottom)

p. 170: Geschwister-Scholl-Archiv/SZ Photo (top); Picture-Alliance/AKG-Images (middle), Dirk Bruniecki (bottom)

p. 171: Jürgen Raible/AKG-Images (top); Catherina Hess/SZ Photo (bottom left), Bernd Feil/MIS (bottom right)

p. 173: KZ-Gedenkstätte Flossenbürg (top)

p. 174: Bundesarchiv Koblenz, Bild 183-N0415-363, photographer: Herbert Donath (top); Museum Mödlareuth, Fotoarchiv, photography: BGS Bayreuth, Mediathek des Deutsch-Deutschen Museum Mödlareuth (middle left); Reinhard Kemmether/Picture-Alliance (bottom left); Jürgen Ritter/DPA/Picture-Alliance (bottom right)

p. 175: Nikolaus Brade (top); Museum Mödlareuth, Fotoarchiv, photography: Bayerische Grenzpolizei, Alfred Eiber, Mediathek des Deutsch-Deutschen Museum Mödlareuth (bottom left); Christine Koenig/Picture-Alliance (bottom right)

p. 176: Archiv Gerstenberg/Ullsteinbild (top); Bayerischer Landtag (bottom)

p. 177: Bayerischer Landtag (3)

p. 178/179: Bayerische Staatskanzlei

p. 180/181: Bitter Bredt

p. 182: Matthias Schrader/picture alliance/dpa/dpaweb, Bayerischer Landtag (bottom left); Peter Kneffel/DPA/Picture-Alliance (bottom right)

p. 183: Kim Oliver Gottschalk Photography

p. 184/185: Image Source/Getty Images (spanner); Dieter Stein (Duke Franz); Getty Images (bridal couple and stone lion); KDFB (Ellen Ammann); Martin Ley/Mauritius Images (police sign); Fotolia (laptop); Bayerische Staatskanzlei (lederhose); Getty Images (jar)

pp. 188/189: Airbus, Linde AG, Siemens AG, Allianz AG, Barbara Bonisolli (Hagelkorn), PUMA, Adidas, MAN

p. 190: BMW (1)

p. 194: Duccio Malagamba (top); Hochschule Augsburg (bottom)

p. 195: Henning Koepke (top); Huber H.-B./Laif (bottom left); Dieter Leistner for Gerber Architekten (bottom right)

p. 196: Rick Jannack for Grabow + Hofmann Architekten (top); Rainer Viertlböck/Artur Images (bottom)

p. 197: Max-Planck-Institut für Plasmaphysik, photography: Volker Stege (top left); Svenja Bockhop for Hascher Jehle Architektur (top right); Robert Pupeter (bottom)

p. 198: Caroline Martin (top right); private (left), Amir Roughani VISPIRON (bottom)

p. 199: Image by Füssen Aktuell (top right); private (bottom right)

p. 200: Constantin Meyer

p. 201: Vario Images (top); Andreas Strauß/Look-Foto (middle); Erdwärme Grünwald GmbH (bottom)

pp. 204/205: AKG-Images, De Agostini Picture Lib./AKG-Images, Wikipedia Commons, Regensburgisch Botanische Gesellschaft, Joseph Hauber/AKG-Images, AKG-Images, Bayerische Akademie der Wissenschaften/AKG-Images, IAM/AKG-images, AKG-images, Sam Morris/AP Photo/Picture-Alliance, NMSI/Science Museum/Ullsteinbild, Infocenter Walchenseekraftwerk, Bildarchiv des Mathematischen Forschungsinstituts Oberwolfach/Universitäts-Archiv Göttingen, Ullsteinbild, AKG-Images (from left to right)

pp. 206/207: United Archives/Mauritius Images; Lebrecht Music & Arts/Ullsteinbild; ZF Friedrichshafen AG, Sachs AG/Wikipedia Commons; oil painting: Harald Duwe, reproduction: Hell-Verein, VG Bild-Kunst, Bonn, 2015; Kathrein Werke; Barry Lewis/In Pictures/Corbis; DPA/Picture-Alliance; Stabilo; Playmobil; Apple; Martin Aufmuth/OneDollarGlasses/dpa/Picture-Alliance; MTU Aero Engines AG

pp. 212/213: Lindau Nobel (s/w), Ch. Flemming and R. Schultes/Lindau Nobel Laureate Meetings (all other images)

p. 214: Elias Hassos (top left); 2 Hands/Authentics (bottom left); Chair One/Magis: Tom Vack (bottom right)

p. 215: Atelier Steffen Kehrle (top and bottom); Julian Baumann (middle)

p. 216: Bulthaupt (top and left); Robert Fischer (bottom)

p. 217: Wrongforhay ROPETRICK by Stefan Diez, photography: Jonathan Mauloubier (top); Andreas Müller (bottom)

p. 218: Die Kunstglaser, Rottweil (right)

pp. 222/223: Getty Images (flag); Science Photo Library/Getty Images (iris); loaners: Rudolf Rühle, Bonn, photography: Schwäbisches Bauernhofmuseum Illerbeuren/Tanja Kutter (board game); Getty Images (CO$_2$); Apic/Getty Images (Alzheimer) White House Gift Shop (White House); Heico (goose); Getty Images (rape); Rennwagen (ABT Sport)

pp. 224/225: Siemens AG

pp. 226/227: Wieland Schmidt/www.shapeandform.de, 20th Century Fox Home Entertainment 2012 (small image)

pp. 228/229: Bernd Mueller/Redferns/Getty Images, EXASOL AG (small image)

pp. 230/231: Audi Urban Future Initiative, TU Munich (small image)

pp. 232/233: Jan Greune/Look-Foto; Harald M. Valderhaug, NO-6050 ValderØy – Norway (small image)

pp. 234/235: Gallery Stock, Panthermedia (small image)

pp. 236/237: Audi AG, Kuka (small image)

pp. 238/239: Siemens AG/reprinted from Siemens' Pictures of the Future magazine Poroton (small image)

pp. 240/241: Michael Jungblut, Huber SE (small image)

pp. 244/245: AWR

Imprint

Bibliographic information published by the Deutsche Nationalbibliothek
The Deutsche Nationalbibliothek lists this publication in the Deutsche Nationalbibliografie; detailed bibliographic data are available on the Internet at http://dnb.dnb.de

First published 2015
© 2015 Verlag Schnell & Steiner GmbH, Leibnizstraße 13, 93055 Regensburg
© 2015 Bayerische Staatskanzlei, Franz-Josef-Strauß-Ring 1, 80539 München

English translation and copy editing
Bernd Weiß, www.get-translated.de, in collaboration with Dr. Cynthia Hall and William Soutter.
The Bavarian Anthem by William Soutter

Typesetting
Anzinger | Wüschner | Rasp
Agentur für Kommunikation, Munich

Printing
Erhardi Druck GmbH, Regensburg

ISBN 978-3-7954-2946-1

Printed in Bavaria

Further information on our program at: www.schnell-und-steiner.de

As of December 2014

Bibliography

pp. 26–32:
Bavaria: fifteen hundred years
Bosl, Karl: *Bayerische Geschichte,* Munich, 1990 (7th ed.)

Haus der Bayerischen Geschichte (ed.): *Politische Geschichte Bayerns,* Hefte zur Bayerischen Geschichte und Kultur, Heft 09, Munich, 1990 (2nd ed.)

Hartmann, Peter Claus: *Bayerns Weg in die Gegenwart. Vom Stammesherzogtum zum Freistaat heute,* Regensburg, 2004 (2nd ed.)

Hubensteiner, Benno: *Bayerische Geschichte, Staat und Volk, Kunst und Kultur,* Munich/Rosenheim, 2009 (17th ed.)

Kraus, Andreas: *Geschichte Bayerns. Von den Anfängen bis zur Gegenwart,* Munich, 2004 (3rd ed.)

Prinz, Friedrich: *Die Geschichte Bayerns,* Munich, 1999 (2nd ed.)

pp. 100–111:
Jolly customs in Bavaria
Huber, Gerald (ed.): *Feste. Vom Aperschnalzen bis zum Schlappentag,* Munich, 2013

pp. 134–135 and 146–147:
A matter of opinion!
Roth, Brigitta: *Bayern in Zitaten der Welt,* Munich. 2001

pp. 170–171:
A White Rose for freedom
Diem, Veronika: *Die Freiheitsaktion Bayern. Ein Aufstand in der Endphase des NS-Regimes,* Kallmünz, 2013

Haus der Bayerischen Geschichte (ed.): *Rebellen. Visionäre. Demokraten. Über Widerständigkeit in Bayern,* Edition Bayern, Special Issue 06, Augsburg, 2013

pp. 176–177:
A royal pain! Who's in charge in Bavaria?
Maximilian Graf von Montgelas, quoted after: "Reformen in Bayern", Haus der Bayerischen Geschichte, available at: http://www.hdbg.de/montgelas/pages/hmv40.htm (11.09.2014)

Thoma, Ludwig: *Briefwechsel eines bayerischen Landtagsabgeordneten,* Munich, 1909

Magazines and online publications

pp. 76:
Typically Bavarian
Deutschlandradio Kultur: Der Weißwurstäquator. A geographic reconaissance, available at: http://www.deutschlandradiokultur.de/landgang.1001.de.html?dram:article_id=156619 (20.10.2014).

pp. 100–111:
Jolly customs in Bavaria
Bayerischer Trachtenverband e.V.: "Geschichte des Dirndldrahn", available at: http://www.trachtenverband-bayern.de/dirndldrahn.html (02.03.2015)

Bayerischer Trachtenverband e.V.: "Geschichte des Schuhplattlers", available at: http://www.trachtenverband-bayern.de/schuhplattln.html (20.10.2014)

p. 135:
A matter of opinion!
Süddeutsche Zeitung: "Wochenend-Interview. Dirk Nowitzki über Bescheidenheit", SZ no. 205 (06./07.11.2014).

pp. 178–179:
Bavarian Minister Presidents
Die Welt online, 2007: "Kommentar. Anarchische Bayern", available at: http://www.welt.de/print-welt/article709898/Kommentar-Anarchische-Bayern.html (20.09.2014)

p. 193:
488 billion euros of economic clout
Die Welt online, 2014: "Airport-Ranking 2014. Das sind die besten Flughäfen weltweit", available at: http://www.welt.de/reise/article126335576/Das-sind-die-besten-Flughaefen-weltweit.html (20.09.2014)

Contributing photographers

Our team of young photographers was given the seemingly impossible task of capturing Bavaria and its people as never seen before, from new angles, from all sides and in their moments of magic – task magnificently accomplished!

Kilian Blees (b. 1981)
Natural attractive and devoid of pretence – that's how people seem in Kilian Blees' pictures. The Schlierseeborn photographer succeeds in getting his subjects to shed their inhibitions in front of his lens. He learned his craft at Munich's Academy of Fine Arts – and on his travels through Nepal and Tibet.

Kilian Schönberger (b. 1985)
Born in the Upper Palatinate, Kilian Schönberger knows the beauty of Bavaria's landscapes like no one else. He manages to expose the extraordinary facets of seemingly ordinary scenes, his pictures lending landscapes a mystical quality. A geographer by training, he is a close observer of current changes in the natural and cultural environment.

Manuel Irritier (b. 1986)
from Munich specializes in architectural and cityscape photography. His portfolio includes the modern Munich with its BMW World and Pinakothek der Moderne gallery alongside the Hong Kong skyline. His photographs acquire enormous depth by virtue of the way their clear, modern imagery traces how architecture truly affects its environment.

Steffen Egly (b. 1987)
from Erlangen chooses to focus on people. His outdoor and lifestyle portraits reflect authenticity and joie de vivre. His clever apposition of landscape and protagonists enables the observer to identify closely with and even feel part of his concise photographic studies.

Contributing authors

Hans Kratzer
Every week in the *Süddeutsche Zeitung* newspaper, journalist Hans Kratzer writes a column full of wit and expertise in which he explains terms from Bavarian dialect. Over time, this Lower Bavarian has assembled a veritable treasure trove of words and expressions to help Bavarians preserve their unique dialect.

Dr. Richard Loibl
In his capacity as director of the House of Bavarian History in Augsburg, he is in charge of preserving the collective memories of the Bavarians. As provincial historian, he is responsible for Bavarian state exhibitions and also drew up the concept for the Interactive Museum of Bavarian History due to open its doors in 2018 – on the occasion of the Free State's 100th birthday.

Professor Armin Nassehi
is professor of sociology at Munich's Ludwig-Maximilians-Universität. Born in Tübingen in 1960, the distinguished scholar grew up in Munich, Landshut, Teheran and Gelsenkirchen. Nassehi is involved in the analysis of modern societies and questions of cultural, political, religious, cognitive and scientific sociology.

Roland Pongratz
is a Bavarian folklorist. As Cultural Officer for the district of Regen in eastern Bavaria, he initiated the *'drumherum'* folk music festival. Its 400 or so groups and 50 000 spectators make it one of the largest events in the Bavarian Forest area.

Professor Anthony R. Rowley
is British and has dedicated himself to research into the Bavarian language. He works with a large team of helpers on a Bavarian Dictionary for the Bavarian Academy of Sciences and Humanities. A job for life, as Professor Rowley has now been working on the project for a quarter of a century, and there's still around 50 years of research to be done before the volume is complete.

Peter Seewald
is a Bavarian journalist and writer. After his first meeting with Cardinal Joseph Ratzinger, the later-to-be Pope Benedict XIV, he rejoined the Church. Seewald has written three works in collaboration with Joseph Ratzinger/Pope Benedict, which have been translated into over thirty languages. His portrait of the Bavarian Pope also drew worldwide admiration.

Hermann Unterstöger
has been writing for the *Süddeutsche Zeitung* newspaper for three and a half decades. He became known for his reports on page three and the humorously didactic column *'Streiflicht.'* As the head of the *'Streiflicht'* team, he accepted the Henri Nannen Award in 2005. For his writing style, the Upper Bavarian was awarded the Ben Witter and Ernst Hoferichter prizes.

"Extra Bavariam
non est vita et si est vita
non est ita."

"There is no life beyond Bavaria –
at least, none such."

(Inscription on the outer façade
of Esting castle chapel)